A QUEEN
Waiting On Her *King*

Marlyn Thomas, D.TH

A QUEEN
Waiting On Her *King*

Marlyn Thomas, D.TH

Printed in the United States of America by
T&J Publishers (Atlanta, GA.)
www.TandJPublishers.com

All Bible verses are taken from the New International Version (NIV) and the New Living Translation (NLT).

Cover Design by Timothy Flemming, Jr.
(T&J Publishers)
Book Format/Layout by Timothy Flemming, Jr.
Photography by Porsha Antalan
Hair: Ekeena Smalls
Makeup: Nzinga Imani

ISBN: 978-0-5789961-7-2

To contact the author, go to:

www.MotivationWithDrMarlyn.com
win@motivationwithdrmarlyn.com
Facebook: Marlyn S Thomas
Instagram: @BishopMarlynThomas

DEDICATIONS

This book is dedicated to my Lord and Saviour Jesus Christ. For without Him, I am nothing!

I also dedicate this book to my mother, Monteen Heard who raised me to be a Queen.

And to my son, Kenneth Gaines, Jr., I'm honored God chose me to be your mother. Thank you Kenny for speaking life into me during the darkest season in my life, reminding me that I am a Queen and to never settle for anything less than God's best!

ACKNOWLEDGMENTS

Thank you to my Church family, Life Line Family Worship Center. Thank you for your faithfulness, love and prayers. The best part of my day is knowing I get to serve you as your Pastor. We are Life Line strong! Always Winning Together!!!

To the most amazing family I was blessed to be born into, thank you! You all keep me laughing. You're my shoulders to lean on and the greatest support system anyone could have. I love each one of you. Big hugs!

To my awesome sisters and friends who have cried with me, laughed with me, and above all else, prayed for me, thank you. My life is 'rich' because of your presences.

To my God parents, Pastors Patrick and Dr. Janice Grier, thank you for your unfailing love and for always having my back through the highs and lows, the good and bad. You were there to push me and pray me through. I love you to the moon and back!

And last but definitely not least, thank you to my Spiritual Parents, Apostles Tony and Cynthia Brazelton (Dad and Mom). Words can't express how much I appreciate you for everything you've done for me. You have shown me what God's love looks like, how 'love in action' is expressed, and truly what a King and Queen in marriage is. I love you and I'm honored to be your daughter.

Table of Contents

FOREWORD

In the timely book, *A Queen Waiting On Her King*, you will receive prayers for areas of your life while waiting and discover your identity, know your self worth, discover your gifts and callings, you'll learn to leave the pass life (2 Corinthians 5:17), make wise decisions, love again, become virtuous, prepare you for marriage and help you embrace your future with much hope and great anticipation for what God has ordained for you. You will also discover what it means to wait on your King and not settle for just anyone. Your waiting is not just for a man but waiting on the Lord. In your serving the Lord and seeking Him, you will find everything He has for you will be added onto you (Matthew 6:33).

The title alone, "A Queen Waiting On Her King," reveals how God sees His daughters—as Queens born from royalty. We are the offspring of God (Acts 17:28). Furthermore, "A Queen Waiting On Her King" provides relational insight that, had we known before, would have caused us to avoid many mistakes and pitfalls.

When we scan the relationship spectrum, we find that some people are experiencing anxiety in their relationships, suicidal thoughts, double mindedness, confusion, they feel conflicted, unstable, stressful, and some are experiencing inappropriate relationships while others are pretending to be someone or something they're not. Many are "settling" instead of waiting on God. We say things like, "It ain't that bad. I'm good." In other words, they are just surviving, not progressing. GOD is calling HIS people to MAXIMIZE their relationships, not COMPROMISE in them. What are you looking for?

God is unpredictable in activity but predictable in character. We don't control outcomes. God controls outcomes. When you have unfulfilled expectations, it will lead to frustration. Stop trying to control everything and wait on God. God is waiting on us to give the proper response to His Word: Believe it and receive it!

There are things about ourselves that we all like and dislike. Sometimes we dislike ourselves due to comparrisons we've made to others. Don't compare yourself to others. The enemy is good at pointing out our differences and making us feel like there's something wrong with us when in reality, these differences are what makes us unique. He tries to put value on us based on race, gender, education, looks, economics, etc. He devalues you based on the circumstances of your life, family history, and the likes. You must know that you are valuable. You are to die for! Jesus died for you because you were worth it (John 3:16).

God sees you as priceless and His love for you is priceless. Psalm 36:7 says, "How priceless is your unfailing love, O God! People take refuge in the shadow of your wings" (NIV). Receive His love!

The biggest crime in the world is identity theft. Don't let others or circumstances rob you or define who you are; don't let them determine your worth and value. Don't live based on what others say; live based on what God says. Let the Word define you. We use the Word of God like a mirror and discover who God says you are and what He has for you.

2 Corinthians 3:18 NKJV says, "But we all, with unveiled face, beholding as in a mirror the glory of the Lord, are being transformed into the same image from glory to glory, just as by the Spirit of the Lord." We are to reflect the glory of God. Christ in us the hope of glory (Colossians 1:27).

The enemy wants to give you an identity so he can manipulate and control you. The only way he can manifest is if you give him permission. He's a counterfeit. Your real identity is in God; He expresses himself through you. We were created in His image and likeness (Genesis 1:26).

The book of James shares with us a common problem we have when looking into the mirror (the Word of God); we see ourselves but then forget what we look like and who we are. James 1:23-24 KJV says, "For if any be a hearer of the word, and not a doer, he is like unto a man beholding his natural face in a glass: For he beholdeth himself, and goeth his way, and straightway forgetteth what manner of man he was." Don't allow circumstances and people to define who you are and tell you what you can have. John 17:16 declares, "They are no more defined by the world than I am define by the world" (The Message Bible). Don't forget who you are. You are a Queen!

God has a great plan for your life (Jeremiah 29:11). Before you were born, God had a plan, and He will see to it that His plan for life manifests.

Romans 8:28-30 states, "So we are convinced that every detail of our lives is continually woven together to fit into God's perfect plan of bringing good into our lives, for we are his lovers who have been called to fulfill his designed purpose. For he knew all about us before we were born and he destined us from the beginning to share the likeness of his Son. This means the Son is the oldest among a vast family of brothers and sisters who will become just like him. Having determined our destiny ahead of time, he called us to himself and transferred his perfect righteousness to everyone he called. And those who possess his perfect righteousness he co-glorified with his Son!"

During the years we have known Bishop Marlyn, we have seen her in different stages of her life; we've seen her weather some of the biggest storms. When it comes to relationships, she has learned from the Lord how to handle those challenges while continuing to serve and minister to those around her. It wasn't always easy for her, but with God, "all things are possible." This book comes from a place of experience. Bishop Marlyn has a word that will certainly help you become the godly and successful woman of God you need to be while you Wait On Your King.

—Apostles Tony and Cynthia Brazelton

It's Time To Get Ready

Yes, it's time to prepare yourself for the man God is bringing into your life. God has the perfect man for you. He desires that you have a King. Why? Because you are royalty; you are a Queen.

Let me repeat what I just said: "You are a Queen!" You aren't an ordinary woman; you are a daughter of the Creator of Heaven and Earth. You deserve the best. And it is important that you know that. However, you have to prepare for where God is taking you and the man He is bringing into your life. That's why I wrote this journal, and that's also why you currently have it in your hands. It's not by coincidence that you're reading this book; it's by divine providence. God is getting you ready for the man He has set aside for you.

In this journal, I share my thoughts and experiences and also revelation pertaining to relationships and personal development from the Word of God. I pray that you allow these revelations to sink within and give you a new perspective. Furthermore, there is a journaling section at the end of each chapter. I encourage you to write down your thoughts. Engage in self-reflection and ponder over the information provided for each day. As you participate in this process, you will find yourself growing as an individual.

Yes, you must grow personally so that you can attract the type of man God wants to send you. When you let God heal your heart from the pain of yesterday and transform you from the inside out, you will become the type of woman that attracts a King.

Let this book be your guide into becoming that woman. Let me coach you through the pages of this journal. Let's get started.

DAY 1

TRUSTING GOD'S TIMING

ONE OF THE WORSE FEELINGS ONE CAN experience is the feeling of not being in control. We all like to think and believe we have the power to control life. When things happen that we don't plan for or our plans don't pan out as expected, we panic, worry, and become overcome with anxiety. Some of us plummet into depression. We suddenly feel like our lives are spiraling out of control or falling apart. At that point, we enter into what's called desperation.

That is exactly where I was at one point in my life. That feeling of hopelessness settling in the pit of my stomach, confused and perplexed, my body trapped in a cocoon of nervous energy. I felt the compulsion to do something, but I didn't know what. That led to even more frustration. The clock on the wall was ticking away. I could hear the tick-tock, the countdown to what I imagined was a dreadful end: a life-time of missed opportunities, the biggest of them being the opportunity to experience a lasting and fulfilling love.

If you're in that place, let me stop and put your mind at ease right now. You never were, nor will you ever be, in control of life. You couldn't control where you were born, to whom you were born, where you grew up, what happened to you as a child, nor can you control the circumstances of your life today. You don't even know what tomorrow holds, so how can you presume to think you can control tomorrow?

Smart people try to control circumstances and people, but wise people simply trust the one who is in control with their lives. Do you want to be smart, or wise? That's the question. I discovered at some point that it was better to be wise than smart, and so I let go of the anxiety and fear and relinquished all control over my life and situations to God. And that's when I got my mind back and began to experience a peace, joy, freedom, and an assurance I'd never experienced before.

I discovered during this time in my life that God is a God of timing. He has things set in His timing. He knows when and how to bless us. He knows when to move. He knows when we're truly prepared for certain things, and He knows how to prepare us. He never guaranteed me that He was going to move in my timing, according to my will; what He did promise me was He would see to my every need and cause all things in my life to work according to His will—and for my good. That's when I sat back and relaxed and began to trust that He was in complete control.

You've probably heard it said before that when you go looking for love, it evades you, but when you stop looking for it, that's when it finds you. In a sense, that's true.

But I'd like to put a spin on that saying: When you try to make things happen, God will step back and let you wear yourself out, but when you stop trying to make things happen and trust God, that's when He'll make things happen for you. And trust me, God can do what you and I can never do.

When I think about the timing of God, I think about several people in the Bible, one being Sarah. In Genesis 17:16, God promises Sarah and her husband Abraham a child. At the time, Sarah was already beyond the age of childbearing, which made that promise seem laughable. It would take a miracle for her to get pregnant at that point.

And yet, God promised her a child.

After the promise, years passed. Sarah still wasn't pregnant, though she and her husband tried repeatedly to conceive. Desperation set in, and that's when Sarah hatched a plan. She went from trusting God to trying to manipulate and control circumstances, which is what led to an even bigger problem. She came up with the plan to have her husband sleep with her servant, Hagar, and conceive a child with her, which they'd adopt and raise as their own. Of course, this backfired, as you'd expect. Anytime you give your man away to another woman... Yeah. You're just being plain foolish.

And yet, desperation will make you do the most foolish things. You'll date people you know you shouldn't date, sleep with people you have no business being with, say yes when you know you should say no, go places you know you shouldn't go, put yourself in positions you should never be in, and agree to things you'd never agree to when in your right mind.

Desperation is Satan's greatest opportunity to whisper into our ears and derail our lives through bad decision-making.

After making a terrible mess of their lives due to their own efforts, God finally made good on His promise to bless Abraham and Sarah with a child. By this time, Sarah was ninety-years-old and Abraham over one-hundred-years-old. God made them wait until the only option left for them was a miracle. God didn't move when Abraham and Sarah wanted Him to move. God had a bigger plan in mind.

God will make you wait until your heart is healed of some past wounds. He made me 'wait' until I had gone through a process of deliverance and transformation in my life and was now the type of woman prepared for the type of man He has in store for me. And during the process of waiting I have to avoid comparing my situation to others or becoming antsy about being in a relationship..

Never compare yourself to someone else, especially when you're in a season of preparation for greater in your life. God doesn't just want to bless you; He wants to give you His best. But if you move ahead of Him and act out of haste, you'll find yourself settling for something that isn't God's best for you. You'll jump for the first guy that winks his eye at you and offers you some sweet words. It probably wouldn't matter that he's all wrong for you, that he doesn't have the right vision, that he doesn't even have a spiritual foundation, that he doesn't even have a basic foundation of morality, doesn't want to work and pay bills, doesn't respect himself and others. Hey, you'd probably stoop so low as to make arrangements to be with a married man, resigning to be that "chic on the side," the other woman, "that hoe over there" (a.k.a. "a T.H.O.T.") just to say you have somebody in your life.

When you know you're God's daughter, you know you're the King's daughter, and as a daughter of the King, only royalty will due for you. You don't settle for that which is common because you aren't common. You're royalty. In fact, 1 Peter 2:9 says it:

> "But ye are a chosen generation, a royal priesthood, an holy nation, a peculiar people…"

Royal. Holy. Peculiar. Nothing in there says you are average. Nothing there suggests you were made for average. Quit looking for something that's beneath what God deemed acceptable for you.

Marriage is perhaps the most important decision you'll ever make in your life next to surrendering to Christ. Marriage can either make or break you; it can leave you in the poor house or send you into Prosperity-ville. Marriage can enhance your life or ruin it. More people's lives and careers have been ruined by bad marriages than anything else. That's a decision you don't want to take lightly.

In the old days, young people were expected to marry. It didn't matter if the guy a girl was going out with was bad news; if the two of them had a child out of wedlock, they were expected to get married for the sake of the child. That was one of the biggest mistakes ever made. In many cases, women married men that beat and abused them, even killed them all because they were "expected" to marry just to cover up a sin.

Never make a life-altering decision simply because someone else wants you to. Remember, you're the one that has to live with the decision, not them. It's your life, your future, your body. Wait on God and don't move until He gives you the green light—until He speaks to your heart and tells you to do something. God not only loves you, but He knows the future and wants what's best for you.

Trust in the timing of the Lord.

PRAYER

Heavenly Father, I trust your timing for my life. I know that you are a God of timing. As the Bible says, Your ways are not my ways. In fact, Your ways are higher than my ways. So Father, I surrender to Your will for my life. I relinquish all control over my life and ever circumstance and defer to Your will and judgment. Without You, I can do nothing. Lead me, guide me, and have Your way in my life. I am yours. Forgive me for moving ahead of You and not trusting You. I repent of this and turn my heart back to You. In Jesus name, amen.

DAY 1: TRUSTING GOD'S TIMING

I'M WORTH
THE WAIT

I DON'T KNOW ANYONE IN LIFE WHO HASN'T experienced painful situations. Most of us have experienced things like bullying, abuse, and neglect of some sort growing up. These experiences have a tendency to hammer our self-esteem and make us feel unworthy. If you had parents who neglected to show you unconditional love growing up, you probably grew up questioning your worth and feeling as if you had to perform just to receive love. If you didn't perform well enough, your parents didn't validate you. When you made good grades, scored a touchdown or made the winning shot, achieved some measure of success in life, that is when your mom and/or dad expressed their love and appreciation for you. You then grew up and spent your entire life feeling unworthy and like you have to prove your worth and earn other people's love and respect. Your entire life has been spent in performance mode, and you don't know how to turn it off.

It's funny that a few years ago, a report that came

out revealing that the majority of the top models you and I see on magazine covers, billboards, in commercials and even movies suffer with low self-esteem. They deal with shame. They're ashamed of their bodies although the media glorifies them as glaring examples of perfection. Hollywood celebrities and successful entertainers spend billions of dollars every year on plastic surgery to change the way they look. They don't like their ears, their noses, their lips, their breasts, their butts, the chins, the jawlines, their cheekbones, eyes, etc. They're constantly seeking validation like a hamster on a wheel—ever burning energy but going nowhere. They're constantly fighting to overcome a lie in their heads, that lie being they're not good enough.

No amount of money will make you feel good about yourself when you carry the inner belief that you're not good enough and worthy enough for love and respect. You'll be rich and miserable, and perhaps end up like the slew of celebrities we've seen over the past few years who committed suicide inside of their plush estates. They had the admiration of the world but couldn't find it within themselves to love who they are. The seed was planted in their minds and it took root inside of them, haunting them throughout their lives—I'm talking about the seed of self-doubt and unworthiness.

For you, it might have been abuse and molestation that made you feel unworthy. As you grew older, you wrestled to understand why you were targeted. You blamed yourself for the incident. You beat yourself up for not stopping it, for not being big enough and strong enough to prevent it. You wondered whether or not you deserved to be abused. You currently walk around with a big question mark hanging over your head. Others can see it in your eyes that you don't believe in yourself, that you don't perceive yourself as deserving of love and respect, and that you eagerly crave their validation and attention. The predators pick up on it and run with it, feeding you what you want to hear in order to further use you and damage your heart. You even remain in relationships with abusers because you either tell yourself you deserve to be mistreated or you will never find anything better than what you have. And even if you do decide to move on, your standards are set so low that you settle for that which is beneath you, that which isn't even suitable for you.

The saddest part in this entire story is people who lack respect for themselves tend not to have any standards. They hardly take the time to discover what they like and set boundaries for themselves. They're so consumed with trying to gain other people's attention and acceptance they fail to pay themselves any attention and accept themselves. They don't know themselves, therefore, they don't even know what to accept about themselves.

Again, if you're in that place, let me put your mind at ease. We're all broken people. In one way or another, everyone's life has been marred. Sure, there are those who seem to operate with a profound sense of confidence, but even they carry scars and possess shortcomings. No one is better than another. Furthermore, all of us wrestle with the same crippling disease that not only threatens to steal our destinies and end our lives, but rob our souls of an eternal home in Heaven: sin. Like Romans 3:23 says, all have sinned and fallen short of God's glory. And it's for this cause that God sent us a Savior (Jesus the Christ). Since we're all broken and sin-laden, all of us need fixing. None of us can afford to be confident in ourselves.

I love motivational speeches. They're so empowering. I enjoy listening to empowering messages that talk about the power of the human potential. They pick me up at times when my mind wonders into self-loathing. But I'm also aware of one thing: without God, I'm a mess. You may have confidence in certain areas of your life but lack confidence in other areas. You may be good at certain things but fail in other areas of your life. Some people are public successes and private failures while others are private successes but public failures.

The Bible says,

> "...for we are the true circumcision, who worship in the Spirit of God and take pride in Christ Jesus, and put no confidence in the flesh." (Philippians 3:3, NASB)

There are many verses that warn against becoming proud and thinking of yourself so highly. Some people grow overconfident and believe they have life by the horns only to discover the hard way they are not masters of the universe when life throws curve balls their way and lay them on their backs. You put all of your stock in your looks and then an accident leaves you physically scarred. You put all of your stock in your physical talent and athletic ability and then an accident leaves you crippled and maimed. You prided yourself on your intellect and then you lost your mind due to stress, anxiety, depression, and other illnesses. Now you have to take ten different medications just to function throughout the day. Either this or you have a psychotic breakdown.

Yes, I'm dismantling the notion that you're less than someone else or even better than someone else in this world. I'm doing so because when I talk about knowing your worth, I want you to have a foundational understanding. Your value as a person doesn't come from your parents. They were imperfect people searching for their own worth. They just had you; they didn't create you. God created you. You were fearfully and wonderfully made by Him. You are the workmanship of His hands.

No one can fully control the things that happen to them in this world. The only thing we can control is how we perceive each situation and ourselves. Think about this. You think you've been victimized, what about God? Here's God Himself walking around in the flesh and He gets put on a cross unfairly, beaten within and inch of His life on a whipping post, gets called everything but the Son of God, has His beard ripped out by the roots and his face disfigured during a mock trial at night, and suffers the worse, cruelest abuses ever. And He's God! And yet, Jesus never doubted His worth. He knew who He was and why He came. He knew the people weren't in control of His fate; the Father was. Jesus knew that the Father would not allow Satan to do whatever he wanted to with Christ. And likewise, know that what happened to you didn't kill you; it only made you stronger.

Know that your worth isn't in the things you possess or lost; it's in the purpose God created you to be and the purpose He predestined for your life. You were created in the image of a great, powerful, and loving God, and you were designed for a great and powerful purpose. Everything that happened to you simply made you stronger and produced the compassion and character inside of you needed to operate in that purpose. The only thing you have to defeat is the lie of the devil that tells you that you are defeated, powerless, and useless because of your past. You're powerful in Christ. In fact, you're a giant in the spirit. You are useful and valuable because of Christ—made in His image and likeness and for His glory and purpose. Your life has a meaning. You have a specific destiny to fulfill. You are not defeated. Quite the contrary. You're a survivor! You lived through things others didn't make it through. You came out stronger than you know.

Now assert your worth. Let the devil know he's a liar and that you are worthy! In fact, say it out loud: I AM WORTHY! You deserve respect not because of anything you've done, but because of who God made you. You're a unique specimen created in God's image, so you don't need to prove anything to anyone.

Now, with that understanding, I want you to quit looking to lost people for validation. They don't even know themselves and their God-given destinies, so how can they validate and direct your steps? They can't. They need what you have. They need what God put on the inside of you. They need you to pray for them and help them find God's plan and purpose for their lives.

When you know and understand this about yourself, you'll stop jumping into relationships hoping that your partner will define you and give you meaning and significance. You'll instead realize that you're a catch, a precious treasure they're blessed to have. You won't lose your identity in the relationship because you came with the understanding of why you're there, with a strong and healthy sense of purpose. Whether they accept you or not, you know your value because you know your purpose and identity in God.

Again, who are you? Let me hear it! Say it loud!

"I am a unique specimen created in the image and likeness of God, and I was created for a mighty purpose in this world! I know my mission and my Maker! I have what others need because I was wonderfully and fearfully created by God, knit together in my mother's womb by Him."

Yes, that's who you are. And don't you forget it.

PRAYER

Heavenly Father, I thank you that you have revealed to me my true identity through Your Word. I know who I am now. I am the righteousness of God, created in Your image and likeness. I am the workmanship of Your hands, created for every good work. I was created to win, to succeed, to prosper. My past doesn't define me; actually, it only proves that I am more than a conqueror. Everything the devil tried to use to take me out has failed. I am still here because I have a purpose to fulfill. Father, reveal to me Your purpose for my life. Let me walk in the purpose and identity You have created for me. I surrender to You, and I thank You for Your grace, in Jesus name, amen.

Day 3

Breaking Generational Barriers

The Old Testament addresses a phenomenon known as generational curses. Throughout the Old Testament, God talks about not just cursed people, but cursed bloodlines. He reveals to us that these curses are the true source behind much of the chaos and turmoil plaguing our families and societies. One such reference can be found in Exodus 20:5, where God said,

> "You shall not bow down to them or worship them; for I, the LORD your God, am a jealous God, punishing the children for the sin of the parents to the third and fourth generation of those who hate me..." (NIV).

All throughout the Old Testament, you'll find God promising to punish the children for the sins of the parents "to the third and fourth generation" of those who hate Him. And let me be clear here, God isn't unfair. When God talks about punishing the children for the parents' sins, He is talking about punishing the ones who decide to walk in their parents' footsteps. In Ezekiel 18:19-20, God tells us,

> "'What?' you ask. 'Doesn't the child pay for the parent's sins?' No! For if the child does what is just and right and keeps my decrees, that child will surely live. The person who sins is the one who will die. The child will not be punished for the parent's sins, and the parent will not be punished for the child's sins. Righteous people will be rewarded for their own righteous behavior, and wicked people will be punished for their own wickedness." (NLT)

So, God is not punishing the children for their parents' sins; He's punishing the children for their decision to practice their parents' sins. Children learn from their parents. Many times, parents will train their children to do the wrong things. Many parents teach their children to lie, cheat, steal, be prejudiced and racist, engage in sexual immorality, even commit murder. Children are taught by their parents to worship idols and disregard God's commandments. It is the job of the parent to "train up a child in the way he should go" (Proverbs 22:6, NASB), which means to teach them God's Word and His commandments so that they'll live blessed lives. Sadly, many parents fail to train their children the right way. They instead train them to disobey God and experience curses.

A generational curse is just divine judgement resting over a household due to passed-down sin. Rather than God's favor resting over that home and bloodline, the opposite is the case. And since sin is Satan's jurisdiction, it opens the door for demonic spirits to plague that household and carry out a campaign of death and destruction in that bloodline. An example of this is found in Genesis chapter four. There is found the story of Cain, the first murderer in the Bible. Cain murdered his brother Abel out of jealousy. God warned Cain that if he let jealousy reside in his heart, he would find "Sin...crouching at the door [of his heart], eager to control you" (NLT). Cain would open up the door of his heart to the demonic if he didn't deal with his anger. Unfortunately, Cain allowed his anger to lead him to murder, and he also passed that curse down to his descendants. In verses 23 and 24 of that chapter, we find one of Cain's descendants (Lamech) committing murder. It reads,

"One day Lamech said to his wives, 'Adah and Zillah, hear my voice; listen to me, you wives of Lamech. I have killed a man who attacked me, a young man who wounded me. If someone who kills Cain is punished seven times, then the one who kills me will be punished seventy-seven times!'" (NLT)

Like father, like son.

Now, what does all of this have to do with preparing yourself for your future King? It has everything to do with it. Before God sends that King into your life, He will work on your heart to heal it from the wounds of the past and work on your mind to correct what several counselors refer to as stinking thinking. You may have been trained the wrong way how to think growing up. If you don't deal with that now, it will sabotage your relationship. If your mother disrespected your father and taught you to treat men the same way, you'll disrespect your husband also because that's what you were taught to do. This will lead to big problems up the road. If you were raised by emotionally unavailable parents who never showed you the proper love, respect, attention, empathy, and compassion you needed in order to grow into a emotionally healthy and mature person, then the effects of that neglect will show up in your marriage and cause a rift between you and your husband. You'll have trouble communicating your needs and feelings to him, will be overly judgmental and critical of him, will fail to lend the emotional support he needs to handle stressful and painful situations, and will certainly end up driving him away and quite possibly into the arms of another woman. If you don't deal with your own insecurities now, you'll project your fears onto your husband and accuse him of being unfaithful at every turn. You'll communicate distrust in him while shutting off your heart in the relationship, afraid of being vulnerable and experiencing hurt. If all you saw growing up were parents fighting and bickering over everything, parents who disrespectfully called one another out of their names, even physical violence in the home, chances are you've been traumatized and taught through their example the wrong way to communicate. This is why some parents call their children out of their names and abuse them—they were raised in abusive environments.

They learned the wrong way to do things and inadvertently passed on the curse by following such bad examples.

God doesn't want you to pass on generational curses; He instead wants you to pass on generational blessings. But the first step is to recognize the habits, thought processes, beliefs, and challenges you face in your own life. You must first become aware of these things and let God heal you from them and change you within. No, it won't be easy, and it won't be quick, but it's necessary. God desires to transform your thinking so you operate just like Him in this world: walking in love and exemplifying the fruit of the Spirit (Galatians 6).

It's what you don't know that's killing you. It's the things you aren't aware of that are controlling you subconsciously. That's how generational curses work—they control you on a subconscious level. You aren't even aware of how you talk to people, how you misuse them or manipulate them, how you mistreat them and make them feel neglected and abused. You are not aware of the fact that you're harsh and judgmental towards others, that you see the world through a dirty lens and view everyone as being out to get you. You don't even notice that you say the meanest and harshest things when you get upset, that your tongue is sharper than a knife and you wield it freely when irritated. You don't even notice that you talk like your mother and respond to stressful situations like your father, both of whom are divorced and are abusive. And then we can take it even further. You haven't even noticed that you tend to go from man to man just like your mom, or turn up the bottle like she did in an attempt to escape life's problems. You worry like your mother, stressing over the smallest things, making a big deal out of nothing because you're a chronic worrier. You smoke cigarettes to calm your nerves, distract yourself with substances and sex, put off responsibilities by overindulging in the clubs and other activities, battle the same sicknesses as your parents, deal with the same mental issues, the same struggles, the same temptations, and more. You don't see these things in yourself, namely because you're afraid to look in the mirror. But you must. You must look in the mirror and take an honest look at yourself.

There's a Bible verse that explains the importance of examining yourself. It reads:

"For if we would judge ourselves, we would not be judged." (1 Corinthians 11:31, NKJV)

If we take time to examine ourselves, we'll prevent a lot of bad habits from sabotaging our relationships and ruining positive opportunities. The way a curse is broken is through open and honest acknowledgment of the habits, addictions, and tendencies you have. You have to be honest with yourself. We all have iniquities we battle with. We were all raised by imperfect people. So now is the time to do the work, the work of self-reflection and introspection. We have to ask the Holy Spirit to be our guide in this matter and take us back into our pasts so that we can identify the snares Satan set for you that have caused our lives to be stagnated. It is critically important that we avoid jumping into a relationship while unprepared mentally. Furthermore, when God does bring up the hidden matters of the heart that are affecting you subconsciously, don't just sit there and pray about them. Get up and find a good counselor to talk through these things. Many emotional wounds from your past will only be healed as you open up about them and bring them to the light in a non-judgmental environment. That is why I prescribed seeing a therapist and not talking to friends and family who'll most likely be biased in their perceptions.

Next, after you've acknowledged the issue, it's time to repent. You break generational curses by repenting of the sin or sins that gave authority to the devil over your household and bloodline. Perhaps your parents made an agreement with Satan through witchcraft, voodoo, Santeria, Wicca, or any other form of the occult, and this has opened up your bloodline to spiritual deception and strong demonic activity. Well, you can shut that door and bring an end to that curse immediately by renouncing that agreement over your life and family and the repenting of that sin. You don't have to allow passed down sins, iniquities, and curses to dominate your life. You can put a stop to them through repentance.

The word repentant means "to turn away from." Simply put, you must turn away from the sin that keeps letting the devil into your home. Is it a sexual sin? Is it an addiction? Is it the occult? Is it abusive behavior? Whatever it is, ask the Holy Spirit to help you stop it and then work towards building positive habits in its stead. The Holy Spirit will help you and empower you to discontinue whatever it is. Just call upon Him with a sincere heart. Let God teach you through His Word the correct way of doing things. He'll teach you through His Word the right way to talk to others, the right way to resolve conflicts, the right way to handle stress and stressful situations, the right way to parent, the correct way to view your husband, and more. If you want to break the generational curses operating in your life today, say this prayer:

PRAYER

Dear Heavenly Father, I come to you today to ask for Your forgiveness for any sins I've committed knowingly and unknowingly. I pray that You give me a clean heart and the right spirit. Thank You for Your Spirit, who is my guide. Your Spirit is the one who searches out my heart. He knows everything that's inside of me. He knows my every thought and desire, my every iniquity and temptation, my every weakness and shortcoming. I surrender these things to You today. I bring my household and bloodline under your authority today and I repent for the sins of my parents and ancestors. I denounce any and all agreements they made with the enemy and declare that today the curse has ended. Today, generational blessings are established in my life and bloodline. Holy Spirit, bring to my awareness any wrong thinking and wrong behaviors in my life. Teach me how to do things Your way. I thank you today that You are transforming me from the inside out, in Jesus name, amen.

DAY 3: BREAKING GENERATIONAL BARRIERS

DAY 3: BREAKING GENERATIONAL BARRIERS

Day 4

Learning From Your Past

ALL OF US HAVE A PAST WE'D LIKE TO FORGET or erase. I don't know how many times I sat back and wished to myself that I had a time-machine. I'd go back and undo a lot of things I did and correct all of my wrongs. For example, if I had a time-machine, I'd go back to the time when I was a fourteen-year-old girl. I'd just grown out of the childhood phase of playing with dolls. As with many girls whose fathers are absent in their lives, I was desperate and searching without realizing it. I was more vulnerable emotionally than I knew, open to the charms of boys who knew how to sweep a girl off of her feet. And one did.

It all happened so fast. One minute I was staring into the eyes of a boy who I thought would be the love of my life, and the next minute I was in a hospital room giving birth to my first child. I was now a teenage mother. My life on hold. My future in question. I was feeling uncertain, scared, filled with worry and fear over what my life would become now.

Let me stop and clear something up. I don't regret having a child, but I regret getting pregnant so soon. If I knew then what I know now, I would have waited until I got married before conceiving a child. I would have laughed off that boy's charms, understanding they were just that: the charms of a boy, a kid who didn't quite understand the seriousness of his actions and wasn't ready for the responsibility that came with them.

Since then, I've gone on to make a ton of other mistakes in my life—bad decisions when it came to relationships, when it came to life-choices, even bad decisions when it came to ministry. I've made mistakes I wish I could take back. But there's no going back in time. Whatever is done, is done.

It's important to note that there is no time-machine that can turn back the hands of time, so stop looking for one. The past is the past. The only thing you can do at this point is either learn from the past or allow it to bury your future. Unfortunately, most people let their pasts bury their futures. They remain buried under an avalanche of guilt, shame, remorse and regret, singing the song Would'a, Should'a, Could'a. They focus all of their attention on what they lost, the opportunities they missed, the things they didn't see coming, the problems they didn't solve, the people they allowed to get the best of them, and the things that were beyond their control. They keep a win-loss record and unfairly deduct points from the win category. They overlook the fact that they didn't lose everything, they did capitalize on opportunities, they did solve some complex problems in life, they do have those moments where they stood up for themselves and demanded respect, and that only God is in complete control. In fact, if they were to be honest with themselves, they have more wins than losses, they've experienced more times where they got it right than got it wrong.

However, regarding what to do with the past, don't let it bury you; learn from it. Use it as a stepping stone, as an opportunity to grow and develop personally. Accept the fact that we are learning and growing every day of our lives, and we learn and grow from painful experiences. Remember when as a child your mother told you not to touch the stove while it was hot? Well, you snuck and did it anyway. And what happened? You learned—you learned never to touch a hot stove again. Pain grew you up; it taught you a valuable life lesson. Well, the same is to be said about the past—it is designed to grow you up and teach you valuable life-lessons. Allow it to do so.

Your value as a person isn't diminished by your mistakes; it actually increases because of them. As you learn from mistakes, you become wiser, smarter, and stronger. As a woman who has made a ton of mistakes, I stand before you today a strong, vibrant, understanding, confident woman because of the mistakes I've made. When I ended the pity-party and chose to evaluate every mistake I've made, taking a look at what I did wrong, at my wrong thinking at the time, taking a look at what was going on inside of me that caused me to end up in the situation I was in, that's when I began to deal with the things inside of me that needed to be dealt with. From there, I began to grow.

Okay, you had a failed marriage that ended in divorce. You ended up with an abusive partner who took you for granted and damaged your self-esteem. You lost your family. Trust me, I understand. The thought of these things are eating you alive, slowly hacking away at your sense of confidence. Stop it! Take the time to examine your thought process then and pinpoint the error of your logic. Take time to examine the wounds in your soul that caused you to be so susceptible and vulnerable to the type of abusive situation you found yourself in. You might need to sit down with a licensed counselor to sort through this—sit with someone that can walk you through the steps of resolving past traumas and regaining the confidence you lost. This will not only expedite the process of healing and restoration in your life, but it will increase the likelihood that you're going about recovering the right way.

It's time to learn, grow, and become the you you're supposed to be. Quit running from and hiding your past and learn from it. It's your stepping stone; use it.

PRAYER

Heavenly Father, I thank you today that my past doesn't dictate and control my tomorrow. I am not a victim of the past; I am a victor. Through all I've experienced and encountered that should have taken me out, I'm still here. I'm here because of your grace and mercy. Lord, I choose to learn from my past and grow from it. Guide my thinking so that negative emotions such as self-pity, regret, shame, and discouragement don't take root in my soul. I surrender completely to you that you may take what the devil meant for evil in my life and use it for my good. For I know that all things work together for the good of them that love you and are called according to your will. I thank you that my past, present, and future are all yours. Have your way in my life this day, in Jesus name I pray, amen.

____

____

____

DAY 5

How Will I Know He's The One?

THIS IS PERHAPS ONE OF THE BIGGEST questions on the minds of single ladies everywhere. Every woman ponders this question in her heart when searching for a partner, and understandably so. If you marry the wrong person, this can cost you dearly. Marrying the wrong person can have a negative impact on your mental and emotional health, your financial health, and even your spiritual health. The Bible warns us not to "be unequally yoked" with people who aren't heading in the right direction in life, and with those who aren't good for us. So how can we know beyond a shadow of a doubt that "the right one" is standing before us?

First, you'll know the right man is standing before you when all that you've prayed for is standing before you. Let me clarify. The Bible tells us in Psalm 37:4, "Take delight in the LORD, and he will give you your heart's desires"

(NLT). What does the phrase "delight in the Lord" mean? It means to "take pleasure in"; it also means "to be soft or pliable." In other words, delighting in God means to spend time with Him, enjoying His presence, loving His Word, building an intimate relationship with Him. When you fall in love with someone, you love and enjoy being in that person's presence. They're all you think about. You light up when you see them. You find yourself on the phone with them all night, even falling asleep while on the phone with them. That's what it means to take delight in someone.

Taking delight in God is more than going to Him in prayer about something that you want. Think about it: would you appreciate having someone in your life who only calls you when they want or need something? They never check on you just to see how you are doing. They never give anything. They don't contribute to your life in any way. All they do is take, take, take. Well, that's how we treat God. We don't thank Him for the things He's done for us and given us. We don't spend time with Him just to be with Him. He's in love with us but we're not in love with Him; we just want to use Him without any consideration to His wants and needs. But what God wants is for us to love Him, to appreciate His presence; to come to Him not simply when we want or need something, but just to love on Him. He wants to know we genuinely love Him and are not simply trying to use Him.

So, delighting ourselves in God is key to finding the right man for you. How so? Well, when we delight ourselves in God, the Bible tells us He will give us our hearts' desires. What does that mean? Some believe it means God will give you whatever you want; however, there is another translation of this that says, when we delight ourselves in God, He will place the right desires in our hearts—the desires He wants us to have. That's what I believe this verse is saying.

Sometimes we desire things that are not in God's will for our lives. Some people desire things that don't even belong to them. For example, a woman can have a desire for another woman's husband. Do you think God will grant that woman her desire? Of course not! What God promises to do in our hearts when we spend time with Him and make our hearts soft in His hands like clay is transform them, reshape them, and place inside of them the things that belong. The more time we spend with God, the more He transforms us from the inside out. So by the time the right man does come into our lives, we would have transformed into the right woman for him.

You see, sometimes we want perfection to come into our lives but we aren't willing to be the perfection someone else desires. It's unfair to desire a man who'll cater to all of your needs and be everything you've ever wanted but you're unwilling to cater to his needs and be everything he's ever wanted. Therefore God has to transform you so that you'll be the answer to someone else's prayers also.

With a new mind, with a new heart that has been transformed, your priorities and values will shift from selfishness, materialism, and purely carnal interests to more meaningful, lasting, God-centered things. You'll find yourself becoming more concerned with things such as character, purpose, one's spiritual walk and relationship to God, and other similar things. Now I'm not saying you won't be concerned about his looks and whether or not he has a job;

what I am saying is character will take precedent over looks and God's divine purpose and will will take precedent over money. Looks will change and fade with time, and money can be lost in a moment and without warning. There is no such thing as job security—companies can close their doors at any moment as we saw in 2007 during the Great Recession. Our only real security is in walking in the will of God and being under His protection and guidance.

The person God sends you will be spiritually compatible with you. In other words, they'll have what you need to fulfill your God-given purpose and you'll have what they need to fulfill their God-given purpose in life. You don't want a man that will hinder you from doing and becoming all God has called you to do and be; instead, you want a man who'll get behind you and push you into your calling while allowing you to push him into his. So many women have married out of desperation rather than praying, spending time with God so that He could transform them from within and reshape their values, priorities, and perceptions, and because of desperation they went for biceps and abs and big bank accounts only to find themselves feeling smothered and stifled by men who fight against God's presence and will in their lives. After a while, these women start to feel suffocated and grow desperate to get out of their relationships. They didn't want to wait on God. They were too impatient to let God bring the right man into their lives.

Take time today and delight yourself in God. Before seeking to fall in love with a man, spend time falling in love with Jesus. He will send you a man after His own heart, one that will love you the way He loves you.

PRAYER

Heavenly Father, I thank you for your Spirit, who is my guide. Holy Spirit, guide my heart and mind so that my desires align with the perfect will of God for my life. I surrender to you today and ask that you give me a clean heart and the right spirit. Lord, you told me in your word that when I delight myself in you, you will give me the desires of my heart, and that when I commit my works over to you, you will establish my thoughts. Today, I turn to you and give you all of me. Fill me, use me, and transform me. Give me the mind of Christ that I may exemplify your wisdom and character throughout this day. Lord, I thank you that whomever you choose to send into my life will also exemplify Godliness and Godly wisdom also in their life. For you want the best for me. You desire that I be equally yoked with a man who is walking close to your heart and in your will. So today, I thank you for my future King and the discernment to recognize him when he comes. I thank you for this in Jesus name, amen.

DAY 5: HOW WILL I KNOW HE'S THE ONE?

DAY 6

THAT'S MY SONG

I'M SURE YOU REMEMBER THE DAYS WHEN YOU USED to hang out at the club. While there, you'd find yourself jamming to the music. But then, there was that one song that once the DJ put it on you had to get on the dance floor. You gladly exclaimed, "That's my song!" You didn't care who was looking or what anyone thought about you at that moment; you were wrapped up in that song like it was a blanket, forgetting about all of the cares of this world. That song was your little piece of heaven, a consolation for all of the pain you endured.

What did you feel when that song was on? You felt pleasure, a sense of euphoria; you found yourself in a zone where no one and nothing could get the best of you. You were doing you. Everyone and everything else could wait. You found your own rhythm and then put the world on pause.

Well, when I talk about finding your own song, I'm not merely talking about music; instead, I'm talking about finding your own rhythm in life. What's your rhythm? What's your flow? What kind of things do you enjoy?

What gives you a sense of satisfaction? If you don't take the time to learn and discover what moves you and makes you happy, you'll simply lose yourself in someone else's world only to frantically search for a sense of self later on.

Establish a set of habits and routines that satisfy you. Find out what are your favorite restaurants, your favorite places to hang out, your favorite activities to do. Do you like to be adventurous? Do you enjoy hiking, skiing, white water rafting? Do you like to travel? Or do you enjoy riding your bike on bike trails on the weekends? Do you love going to the gym and toning and sculpting your body? Is cooking your thing—a therapeutic exercise you enjoy? Or is there a certain convention or event you attend every year like the Super-bowl, a workshop, or festival?

Find your rhythm now.

In the Bible, there's the story of Ruth. Ruth was a young Moabite woman who was the daughter-in-law of Naomi. Both Ruth and Naomi's husbands died. Ruth chose to follow Naomi back to her hometown, unwilling to leave her all by herself. At the time, Naomi was taking her loss very hard; she wasn't coping very well.

While living with Naomi, Ruth began working, gathering grain along with others in a field that belonged to a wealthy man named Boaz. Ruth was in her zone, in her rhythm. She was busy serving Naomi when Boaz noticed her. Ruth wasn't sitting around waiting for Boaz; she was busy working, serving, doing what God placed in her heart to do. And when you get busy doing what God has placed in your heart to do (flowing in your rhythm), that's when someone will undoubtedly notice you and take interest in you.

Researchers have discovered that when it comes to attraction, most people report that their partners look the most attractive when they're doing the things that bring the most joy into their lives. It's when they're in their zone, flowing confidently and freely, that they're the most attractive...and sexy.

Find your rhythm. Find your song. Find yourself and what you love to do, then you'll find yourself becoming the object of someone else's obsession. And you won't lose yourself in someone else's world.

PRAYER

Heavenly Father, I thank you that you made me unique. You made me a one-of-a-kind individual. All of the passions, talents and abilities I possess, you placed inside of me. I embrace who you made me and denounce any ungodly wants and desires that are out of alignment with your will for me. Father, this day, give me my daily bread. Give me a revelation of your will today and show me my divine assignment. Furthermore, teach me how to rest and relax in you and enjoy the little blessings you continuously send my way. Teach me how to focus on the good things you're doing as opposed to the negative things occurring in my life. You designed me to do great things in life and to experience great joy while doing that which you custom made me to do; therefore, today I say yes to your will and plan and pray that you teach me how to focus on and be productive in those things you've predestined for my life. I ask this in Jesus' name, amen.

DAY 7

WHAT I LEARNED FROM BASKETBALL

I'M QUITE SURE YOU'RE FAMILIAR WITH THE GAME of basketball, but if you're not, let me fill you in. In basketball, there are two opposing teams facing off against one another. There can only be five players representing each team on the court at one time. These five players must fill five key positions: point guard, shooting guard, small forward, power forward, and center. Each position has a responsibility. In order for the team to win, each player must be in their proper place, fulfilling their individual role.

In basketball, a team will lose a game when its players fail to do their parts. The point guard may do a good job of dribbling the ball down the court, but if the center isn't in place or the power forward or small forward is in the wrong spot, then the point guard won't have anyone to pass the ball to. Regarding defense, if the center isn't in place, then the other team will most likely score every single time they get the ball because there's no one in the paint to block the opposing team from scoring inside the paint.

Having the right people in place is the key to success in the game of basketball.

Needless to say, I was an athlete—a basketball player during my school days. I loved the game—and still do today. I may not play the game today, but I'm still a fan and a student of it. Basketball has taught me many life lessons, some of which apply to relationships. One of the biggest lessons it taught me is that there are some people who're serious players in the game and some who aren't. Some people just enjoy playing casually, just for fun. These aren't the people you want on your team—they're not serious. You want a serious player, one who studies the game, knows the rules, understands the positions, and dedicates himself to the game.

Life is like a game and our success in life is determined by the people we surround ourselves with. If we surround ourselves with "casual players" who just want to have fun but not take anything seriously, then we'll lose. The same can be said about finding love—it's very important that you weed out those who're not serious about a relationship from those who're serious. Don't waste your time with people who don't want a committed relationship but just want to play games. Some people prefer a friends with benefits arrangement where they get to enjoy all of the benefits of marriage without the struggle, toil, hard work, and commitment that comes along with it. That's selfish, and it's why people who tend to engage in sex before marriage tend not to last together after getting married—they were more focused on serving themselves than one another. When selfishness is the foundation of your relationship, it won't last. As humans, we gain the greatest sense of joy and fulfillment when we serve other people as researchers have observed. We can never feel fulfilled when we focus only on having our wants and needs met. Marriage is about serving another and meeting their needs while they are serving you and meeting your needs. Only serious-minded people are concerned with serving others above themselves.

The purpose of God for your life is going to require a team. You must know where the people in your life fit. Not everyone is marriage material—some guys might simply be good friends or colleagues. Not every man you run into and vibe with well is meant to be in your bedroom—they may not be compatible with you in certain ways nor have the mind-set that's needed to be in that type of relationship. Some people come into our lives only for a season to aid and assist us in different assignments and tasks God has given us; they're not meant to stay. You have to be okay with that. God may have them on a different path, and should you get romantically tied up with them and then find the relationship drifting apart, that might be divine intervention pulling the two of you apart. God knows who's supposed to only be a point guard (someone meant to get something important to you in a certain season) and who is supposed to be at the "center" of your heart. God knows who's designed to remain outside of the paint and who needs to be inside the paint. Shooting guards don't make good centers, and power forwards don't make the best point guards. Know who belongs where in your life. The best way to make this discovery is to ask God to help you discover where each man that comes into your life fits. He'll help you to sort things out, and will certainly help you to weed out the ones that are there to waste your time.

If, by some chance, you notice people dropping out of your life, don't be alarmed—there's nothing wrong with you. It's just God building the right team around you.

PRAYER

Heavenly Father, I thank you that you have made me strong and given me confidence. I am able to make good decisions for myself because you have given me your wisdom. I thank you that you are ordering my steps and preparing me for greatness, and you are sending the right people into my life while removing those who are not designed to be a part of my life and journey. Thank you for giving me the wisdom to deal with each person in my life and to know what their role and assignment is in my life. Also break any and all spiritual soul ties to individuals who are not my soulmate. Lord, I choose to do things your way. I thank you for the grace to live the way you intended for me to live this day, in Jesus name, amen.

DAY 7: WHAT I LEARNED FROM BASKETBALL

DAY 7: WHAT I LEARNED FROM BASKETBALL

DAY 8

FINDING LOVE AGAIN

THE WORST THING ABOUT EMOTIONAL SCARS IS they make it hard for you to open your heart again. After all, no one wants to have their heart stepped on, ripped apart, or impaled with a knife for a second or third time. One time is enough; at least, that's what most people say. And yet, the interesting thing about love is this: Love brings with it its own share of pain. I'm sure you have heard the old saying, "Every rose has a thorn." Well, love has plenty of thorns waiting to prick you; therefore, proceed with caution and handle it carefully. You're simply not going to enter into a loving relationship without experiencing some pain and disappointment from your chosen partner.

The greatest example of this can be found in our love affair with God. How often do we bring pain to His heart? How often do we neglect to show Him appreciation? How often do we take Him for granted? How often do we sin in His face and then strut off arrogantly as if He should just deal with it and shut up about it? Arrogant. I know. But we do this to Him on a continuous basis. And what does He do in return? Love us even more. God knows that love isn't a risk; it's an investment. The more He loves us, the more He cracks our hard hearts and compels us to love Him back. God doesn't love us because we treat Him fair; He loves us because He knows love is what changes us; furthermore, He loves us because He created us in His image and likeness.

God doesn't shut up His heart out of fear of being hurt by us; He even anticipates our offenses and trespasses. He knows we're going to mess up—that's why He provided for us the gift of grace. Grace covers us as His children. God knows we're not perfect, and therefore, He doesn't expect perfection out of us. How can you expect perfection out of imperfect people? You can't even live perfectly, so why expect others to be perfect? Be like God and forgive and be gracious towards others. Leave room for them to make mistakes; after all, it's through our mistakes that we learn and grow. And don't forget to extend forgiveness and grace to yourself also. Your mistakes didn't kill you, and neither do they define you; they simply refined you and made you wiser. Remember, you can't penalize your current self for what you did in a former season of your life. You're not that person. You have a wealth of wisdom now.

Let your guard down, at least, just a little. Love requires vulnerability to thrive. If you are afraid to open up your heart and be vulnerable with someone, you'll never develop a deep and fulfilling relationship with anyone. Become a risk taker again. Don't allow fear to control you. The Bible says, "There is no fear in love; but perfect love casteth out fear: because fear hath torment" (1 John 4:18).

When you're afraid to love out of fear of being hurt, you'll find yourself living in a state of torment, being controlled by imaginations of what might happen, of what someone might do to you; you'll find yourself being controlled emotionally by your circumstances rather than operating with confidence and assurance of who you are in Christ despite your circumstances. Take the attitude that regardless of what someone says or does to you, you know who you are in Christ and who is the source of your strength (God). You will choose to love regardless of what others say or do because God loves you. You take control of your emotions rather than being controlled by fear and circumstances.

If you're going to find love again, you must let go of the past. If you've gone through a traumatic event or a series of traumatic events that have left you mentally and emotionally scarred, then reach out to a therapist who can walk you into mental and emotional healing. Just do whatever it takes to get pass the past so that you can move forward into your bright future. And know that on the path to healing you're going to have to forgive those who hurt you. Now forgiveness doesn't mean forgetting, it doesn't mean erasing what has been done, it doesn't mean living in denial; furthermore, forgiveness is a process. You may forgive someone in your heart and mind, but that doesn't mean the pain they've caused you has vanished; it is still there. However, given enough time and willingness to let go and move forward, the pain will subside. You'll know when you've forgiven someone when you know longer feel the pain when talking about your experiences.

PRAYER

Heavenly Father, I thank you that you are a healer. You heal wounded and broken hearts. As your Word declares in the 51st Psalm, you are close to them who have a broken heart. You told me to cast all of my cares at your feet because you care for me. As David proclaimed in Psalm 56:8, "You keep track of all my sorrows. You have collected all my tears in your bottle. You have recorded each one in your book." Today, I surrender my heart to you. I give you the hurt, pain, and disappointment that I feel. I won't hide anything from you. You already see it anyway, so I give it to you. Thank you Father for touching and healing my heart as only you can. You've given me your peace, your "shalom". You are making me whole right now, even as I speak. I turn every situation over to you that brings hurt to my heart, knowing that you are not just a healer but a miracle worker. Every person who has ever hurt and wounded me, I place them into your hands. Every loss I've experienced, I thank you that you are healing that internal wound right now. I surrender to you today. You are taking my pain and turning it into purpose, giving me beauty for ashes, double for my trouble. You are blessing me for every tear I shed. You see me. I receive everything you're doing in me and through me today. Lord, I open my heart again, first to you, knowing that you will protect me. I choose to walk in forgiveness today. Furthermore, I bind the spirit of fear and plead the blood of Jesus over my heart and mind. I am not destined to live in the fear of hurt, to live with anxiety and worry. I denounce these things and receive your assurance that no weapon formed against me shall prosper. So fill my heart with your love so that I may walk in love rather than fear and love others the same way you loved me. I pray this in Jesus name, amen.

____

____

____

____

DAY 9

YOUR VIP LIST

EARLIER, I TALKED ABOUT THE GAME OF basketball—about knowing who's on your team. In that chapter, my focus was specifically on men—knowing who's marriage material and who's not, knowing who's just an acquaintance and who's supposed to be your lover. In this talk, I want to go beyond the dating and marriage scene and address everyone that's involved in your life: family members, in-laws, your circle of friends, your peers, colleagues, and more. I want you to examine who's on your VIP list.

Understand that the marriage union isn't the only important relationship in your life. Even while waiting for your King to come into your life, you still have other relationships to tend to; in fact, it's important that you cultivate relationships outside of the marriage. Build strong relationships with your family members now. Never lose sight of the important people in your life outside of the marriage.

One of the signs of an abusive, controlling partner is that they don't want their spouse to form any other relationships outside of the marriage; they want their partners to remain isolated from the outside world. That is a dangerous situation to be in. When you're isolated, no one is able to tell when you're experiencing hardships and abuse, no one can help you when you're in need. In a healthy marriage your spouse should not only encourage you to maintain strong connections with family and friends, but they should seek to establish a relationship with them too. As a couple, both of you should attend family reunions, both of you should get to know each other's set of friends.

Of course, there are certain relationships you need to cut loose once you get married. You need to let go of old flames (boyfriends and girlfriends), and it's important that the two of you teach your family and friends to respect the boundaries around your marriage. Never should a family member be allowed to enter into your home without your spouse's consent, and you shouldn't allow family and friends to bad mouth your spouse in your presence. You must set boundaries and let your friends know that they must respect your spouse as well as you, and that may mean certain things they got away with when you were single they cannot get away with now; certain lines they're not allowed to cross now. Your spouse is number one now. You can't just hang out all night on weekends with your girlfriends now; you're married. You can't flirt around and collect numbers and do the stuff that single women do now, not if you intend to stay married. This is why most marriage counselors advise married couples to hang out with other married couples as opposed to singles.

Aside from family and friends, what other circles are you involved in? Are you active in your church? Instead of just sitting back waiting for Mr. Right to drop out of the sky and into your living room, it's better that you get busy serving in your local church, helping out where you can, devoting your time and energy to things that matter. The Apostle Paul wrote in 1 Corinthians 7:32-34,

> "I want you to be free from the concerns of this life. An unmarried man can spend his time doing the Lord's work and thinking how to please him. But a married man has to think about his earthly responsibilities and how to please his wife. His interests are divided. In the same way, a woman who is no longer married or has never been married can be devoted to the Lord and holy in body and in spirit. But a married woman has to think about her earthly responsibilities and how to please her husband." (NLT)

According to the Bible, once married you won't have the time to devote to the things of God like you do while single. Paul explained that you are violating God's will for couples when you neglect the needs of your spouse and household just to focus on spiritual matters and service in the house of God. Your service to your spouse is your ministry now. Taking care of your children is your ministry now. In fact, in 1 Timothy 5:8, Paul wrote, "But those who won't care for their relatives, especially those in their own household, have denied the true faith. Such people are worse than unbelievers" (NLT). So use the gift of singleness while you still have it. Pour out your time and attention on those who currently need you—that niece, that nephew who needs your guidance, the people God is calling you to on that missionary trip in another country, and more. There are so many relationships you need to build now, so many people who need what God has placed inside of you at this moment.

Currently, take inventory of the other important people in your life besides your mate or future mate. Who are your mentors? Who's pouring into you, guiding and advising you in matters big and small? Do you have a mentor or mentors? As the Bible states, "Plans go wrong for lack of advice; many advisers bring success" (Proverbs 15:22, NLT). It's important that you surround yourself with the right advisers. You need advisers who'll steer you in the right direction regarding how to handle your finances, build a strong marriage, raise children, and more. Even after you get married, you need the right advisers to turn to when conflicts arise—and trust me, they will arise. Turning to the wrong adviser(s) can be deadly; it can lead to the death of your marriage. Seeking advice about marriage from someone who can't keep a marriage or has never been married isn't a good idea. And the same goes for every other area in your life.

Who should be on your VIP list? Besides your spouse, it should be your mentors and advisors, your spiritual covering (pastor), your parents, your children, your loved ones, close friends, business partners (if you have a business), and other people who play a major role in your life, helping you to accomplish the will of God for your life and helping to shape you into the person you need to be.

Haters and negative people who want to hold you back and keep you down, you can scratch them off the list.

PRAYER

Heavenly Father, I thank you for sending the right people into my life to help me accomplish all that you've called me to do. I thank you for divine connections and relationships. I thank you for guiding me and directing my every affair on this earth. I acknowledge that you work through other people, which is why you desire that I touch and agree with the right people. Open my spiritual eyes that I may discern and know who you are sending into my life and who the enemy is planting in my path as a hindrance. Father, keep me humble that I may listen to the sound wisdom and advice you are pouring into my life from the lips of others. I cast down the spirit of pride that causes me to push away those you are sending into my life to help, guide, and instruct me. Lastly, Father, I curse the root of every negative word sown, every negative seed planted into my heart and mind by those with satanic motives. I reject every thought and belief that disagrees with your Word, and cast down every demonic imagination that seeks to sabotage and hinder my progress in you. I thank you for sending intercessors around me, for sending people who share my same vision and are passionate about that which you've birthed in my heart. I thank you that your will is being done in my life this day, in Jesus name I pray, amen.

Day 10

What's Your Credit Score?

OFTENTIMES, WHEN TWO PEOPLE MEET AND start dating, their conversations are usually about things like their favorite foods, activities, and even their future plans. And while these are fine to talk about, at some point in the dating stage it's important to engage in the meatier topics. For example, you should inquire about whether or not your partner wants children, and how many. You should inquire about your partner's expectations regarding sex, household chores, and child-rearing. Most of all, you should inquire about your partner's credit score.

I know this sounds crazy, but trust me when I tell you knowing your partner's credit score matters. A lot. Your credit score may mean the difference between owning a house and renting an apartment, between owning a car and relying on public transportation or Uber; it will determine the quality of your lives together. Trust me, the honeymoon phase will come to an end, and once that happens, life will set in. It's during the after-honeymoon phase that couples find themselves in trouble. And the one thing that causes trouble to land in paradise is money, finances.

Bad credit is tied to the mismanagement of money. Does your partner believe in paying their bills on time? Do they believe in paying people back money that they borrowed? Do they believe in being honest and integral? Do they have a bad name and reputation? Are they maxed out on credit cards? Are they steeped in debt they aren't telling you about?

The worse thing that can happen is for you to get married to someone and then find out after the wedding that the man you've married is tens or even hundreds of thousands of dollars in debt. You see, their debt now becomes your problem. If they're undisciplined when it comes to handling credit cards and meeting financial obligations, the burden will fall on you to settle these matters. Are you ready for that?

Just because he drives a nice car and lives in a nice loft, that doesn't mean he's stable financially. He may be neck-deep in debt but still has the appearance of being wealthy. Check his credit score and you'll find out a lot about his habits, financially and otherwise.

Am I insinuating that people with bad credit have bad character? No. Life happens to us all. People often fall behind in life due to circumstances, many of which are beyond their control. In 2007, people lost their homes and possessions once the Great Recession hit. None of this was in their control. Likewise, people fall on hard times and find their credit scores taking a hit as a result of this. After all, no one can predict the future. But my purpose for bringing up your partner's credit score is so you'll gain an understanding of what you're stepping into before you step into it. You need to know if they have any hidden debts they owe, or if they're even in the position to receive financial loans. Their credit will effect you in every way when it comes to living life. You need to know what battles you're about to face. If your partner is unwilling to engage in that conversation with you, then they're not ready to take the relationship to the next level. They're hiding something. And any marriage that starts off with secrets and lies is one that's doomed for failure.

Don't just look for a man with good credit, but work on establishing good credit for yourself also. It's unfair to look for someone else to bring everything to the table while you bring nothing to the table. Your credit will effect your partner's life also. So let me ask you, what are you bringing to the table? Are you settling your debts and paying back money that you owe? Are you establishing a track record of honesty and integrity? Are you prioritizing properly when it comes to handling your finances? Are you drowning in debt and expecting a man to come into your life to help you bear the load or take it off of your hands? These are the things you need to open up and be honest about with your partner; they are the things you need to get right before you even meet someone.

How's your credit looking?

PRAYER

Heavenly Father, I thank you that you are my provider and my keeper. I thank you that your plan is to bless me and prosper me according to Jeremiah 29:11. You did not create me for poverty and lack. You designed me for abundance, wealth, and favor. Your desire is that my cup overflow with so much favor that it spills over onto the lives of those around me. Today, I come against the spirit of poverty and lack and break any and all covenants I've made with it through the words I've spoken. I cast down the poverty mentality and cast down the spirit of stubbornness, stinginess, and fear. Teach me how to think like an overcomer. Teach me how to be responsible and how to be a good steward over the finances you've already given me. Teach me how to honor you with my tithes and how to sow into your Kingdom through seed offerings. Furthermore, thank you for blessing me with seed money to sow into your Kingdom. As you declared in 2 Corinthians chapter nine, you give "seed to the sower." Also, I thank you that I am free from debt. You said the borrower is slave to the lender, and it's not your will that I be a slave to any man. According to Romans chapter 13, I am to owe no man nothing but to love him. So today, I declare that miracle finances are being released to pay off any and all debts I owe. I thank you that I am called to a debt-free life, and my credit is good. I have favor with both God and man. I receive this today, in Jesus name, amen.

Day 11

Be The First
In Your Family

WHILE YOU'RE WAITING FOR YOUR KING TO come into your life, focus on doing things to improve yourself so that when he comes he'll find that he's acquired a jewel. The Bible says this about a woman who's developed and matured into the woman she's supposed to be: "Who can find a virtuous and capable wife? She is more precious than rubies" (Proverbs 31:10, NLT). When a King looks for a woman, he looks for a Queen, not a girl; he wants a woman who knows her value and worth and has established it, a woman who can add to his life in ways no one else can. That's why it's important that you work on you during this time.

One of the most important things you can do during the season of waiting is set goals for yourself and strive for them. And when I talk about setting goals for yourself, I'm talking about big ones, not small goals that don't require much effort and sacrifice to pull off. Aim to do what has never been done before in your family. It's important that you gain a personal sense of accomplishment and discover your fullest potential even before getting tied down in a relationship. You don't want someone else telling you what you can and cannot do, and you don't want to wait for someone else's validation of you in order to feel important. Setting and accomplishing goals for yourself will give you that much needed boost of self-confidence you need to not feel needy and clingy in a relationship. You'll know that with or without a man, you are still valuable and you can make it.

This truly is a new day. These aren't the days of Betty Crocker where women basically sat at home and tended to the kitchen and household chores while waiting for their husbands to come home from work. These aren't the days of women being confined to one segment of society and told what they can and cannot do. Currently women occupy roles that were once only relegated to men. Women are army sergeants, police officers, political officials, corporate CEOs, professional athletes, top paid actors and entertainers, and even commanders sitting in the Oval Office. Women are bringing more to the table than ever before in our nation. To be honest, this is what the Bible describes as a trait of a virtuous woman:

> "She goes to inspect a field and buys it; with her earnings she plants a vineyard. She is energetic and strong, a hard worker. She makes sure her dealings are profitable; her lamp burns late into the night" (Proverbs 31:16-18, NLT).

This woman is a business woman, perhaps even an entrepreneur. She makes investments into business ventures that turn out to be "profitable". She's buying up real estate and managing properties. She's resourceful and powerful. She's not sitting around waiting for some man to give her a sense of purpose and confidence; she's already pushed herself to the limits and seen what she can do; she's already shattered glass ceilings in her own life. Once married, she's able to bring that same tenacity and fire to her marriage, managing her home and her husband's investments. He knows he has more than a lover; he has a partner who can take what he gives her and multiply it.

Are you pushing yourself beyond your own boundaries? Are you setting high goals for yourself and striving to achieve them? Or are you simply waiting for someone to come along and give you an identity and a sense of purpose?

Right now is your opportunity to accomplish things no one else in your family had accomplished. If no one else in your family went to college, you be the first. If no one else in your family started a business, you be the first. If no one else in your family voted, you be the first. If no one else in your family got thin and healthy and beat heart disease, diabetes, and other illnesses, you be the first. If no one else in your family broke the cycle of poverty, you be the first. If no one else in your family owned their own home, you become the first home-owner in your family. What is it that you can be doing right now to set yourself apart in your family?

Becoming a first means becoming a risk-taker. Abram was a first in his family. God told him to leave his mother and father and go to a far away land, a strange land.

He had no idea where he was going and what to expect once there, but he obeyed God and followed His lead. The Bible calls Abram (later changed to Abraham by God) the father of many nations and the father of the faithful. Why? Because he was willing to obey God and do something no one in his family was willing to do: follow God to new territories, to new heights.

God is trying to take you places you and no one else in your family has gone before. He's trying to do something inside of you that's never been done before in your family. Are you in? Are you willing to take the ride? This will require you to think differently from those around you and to make decisions they won't always agree with and understand. You might lose some friends and have to walk alone for some time. However, the reward is worth it. You will eventually find yourself in a blessed place (Promised Land), experiencing an abundance of blessings. Your cup will overflow with provisions and favor so much so until you'll be able to lift your entire family out of the depths of poverty and impact future generations.

Yes, God wants to do something major inside of you even while you're single. He has plans to bless you and establish something extraordinary inside of you even before someone new comes into your life. Today, ask God to do something new, something that's never been done before in your family through you. And be daring enough to let Him take you there.

PRAYER

Heavenly Father, I thank you today for making me a trailblazer, a groundbreaker. I thank you for opening up doors in my life that no man can shut, and shutting doors in my life that the enemy has been using to infiltrate my life. I thank you for breaking every generational curse of poverty, lack, violence, promiscuity and sexual deviancy, premature death, substance abuse and addiction. I thank you for making me a brand new creation in Christ Jesus. I thank you for using me to establish a new lineage, a line of generational wealth. I thank you for causing my offspring to be strong, bold warriors for the Kingdom of God. I declare the 112th Psalm over my life and household today:

"Praise the LORD! How joyful are those who fear the LORD and delight in obeying his commands. Their children will be successful everywhere; an entire generation of godly people will be blessed. They themselves will be wealthy, and their good deeds will last forever. Light shines in the darkness for the godly. They are generous, compassionate, and righteous. Good comes to those who lend money generously and conduct their business fairly. Such people will not be overcome by evil. Those who are righteous will be long remembered. They do not fear bad news; they confidently trust the LORD to care for them. They are confident and fearless and can face their foes triumphantly. They share freely and give generously to those in need. Their good deeds will be remembered forever. They will have influence and honor. The wicked will see this and be infuriated. They will grind their teeth in anger; they will slink away, their hopes thwarted."

I declare and decree that this word is established in my life this day, in Jesus name, amen.

____

____

____

____

TAKING ADVICE FROM FRIENDS

IN 1 SAMUEL CHAPTER TWENTY-FIVE, THE BIBLE records the story of a woman named Abigail and her husband, Nabal. Nabal was a stubborn man. His wife, Abigail, is described as possessing great wisdom. One day, David, while a fugitive on the run from the maniacal King Saul, sent word to Nabal that he and his men had been protecting Nabal's property from thieves and robbers, and all he asked for in return was a little food and wine—David and his men were practically starving. Rather than being gracious and kind, Nabal, despite having more than enough food and wine to spare, decided to be mean. He sent word back to David, blasting him out and flat out rejecting his request; he did this against Abigail's advice. She tried to get her husband to see the benefit in having David's protection over their property and to show gratitude and kindness to David and his men, but Nabal was too wrapped up into his pride to listen. After Nabal's message got back to David, David determined within himself to raid Nabal's property and kill everyone there, servants and all. David was furious. The only thing that stopped David from carrying out this massacre was Abigail who'd approached David on behalf of her stubborn, arrogant husband and begged for forgiveness and mercy while giving he and his men the much needed food and drink that they needed. Nabal's life was spared because of his wife. However, after discovering David's plan to massacre his entire household, Nabal ended up dying anyway—dropping dead from a heart-attack. And David took Abigail to be his wife.

What's the moral of this story? It's simple: It pays to listen to those closest to you. Had Nabal listened to his wife, he would have lived and enjoyed even greater prosperity and protection; however, his unwillingness to listen to the very one who was closest to him, the one who loved him and truly had his back, cost him dearly.

God placed certain people in our lives to be a guiding light to us. God uses people to speak to us and guide us. While many of us tend to look for someone outside of our midst to give us guidance in important matters, God may have placed the answers we need inside of the people closest to us, the very ones we take for granted. It might be your sibling or child who has the answer you need at the moment, or it may be your parent or even a close friend. The point is you need to be willing to hear those closest to you even if you don't agree with what they have to say. Don't shut them off and discount them.

This stage in your life is crucial to the success of your future marriage. While single, it is important that you focus on the areas in your life that need improving. And who better to let you know what those areas are than those closest to you? Your parents know you better than anyone else. They know your strengths and your weaknesses, the way you handle crises, how you respond to certain situations, and more. Your siblings understand you better than most other people, having grown up with you. Furthermore, your friends can tell you a thing or two about you, but you have to be willing to seek out their honest assessment of you and not get offended. Your friends, if they're honest, will tell you if you're a little too selfish, if you are too sensitive, if you're too needy and clingy; they'll let you know what areas you need to improve in.

Why turn to another for an evaluation of you in the first place? It's because others can see things about you that you can't see. There's an old saying that no one can watch their own back. That's true. Furthermore, as another saying goes, you can't see a parade while you're in it. Simply put, all of us must rely on others to see what we can't see. Having others around to hold you accountable is key. Not only do other people have strengths in areas you don't, but they also see what you don't see, and you're able to see what they can't see.

Ask those closest to you what areas in your life you need to work on. Be prepared for the cold, hard truth. Like the Bible says, "Wounds from a sincere friend are better than many kisses from an enemy" (Proverbs 27:6, NLT). A true friend will tell you the truth even if it hurts, but you have to be willing to put aside your ego, humble yourself, and seek the truth. So ask them. Is it you? Do you have a temper? Do you tend to have a negative, pessimistic attitude? Do you tend to belittle and berate others without realizing it? Do you need to work on your mouth—choosing the rights words to say? Do you tend to hurt others' feelings? Do you need to take better care of your body? Change your wardrobe? Handle conflict better? Be more sensitive? Listen more and talk less? Be more selfless? Stop acting so desperate? Or stop acting so high maintenance?

Ask! That's the only way you're going to hear the truth from those who love you. And in the end, trust that what they're telling you is their perception of you; but if they see you in a certain light, then there's a good chance that others see you the same way. They're providing you with valuable information—revealing to you what others may think of you but are too afraid to mention.

PRAYER

Heavenly Father, thank you for positioning people around me who have your heart and have the mind of Christ. Thank you for sending people into my life to help me remain accountable to you and the plans you've placed in my heart. Thank you for those who are in my life that are speaking to the destiny you've planted in my spirit. Give me the wisdom to be humble and the discernment to know and recognize when you are speaking to me and dealing with me through others. Furthermore, Father, give me the humility to work on the areas of weakness that you are highlighting in my life through those you've placed in my life. You chastise those you love; therefore, I receive any and all correction you are sending my way. I denounce the spirit of haughtiness and cast down its works in my life and receive the humility to hear and adhere to sound wisdom, guidance, advice, correction, and rebuke. I thank you for it today in Jesus name, amen.

DAY 13

AM I MENTALLY PREPARED FOR MARRIAGE?

ONCE UPON A TIME, THERE WAS A BEAUTIFUL girl named Cinderella. She had a wicked stepmother and two wicked step-sisters who treated her cruel. Poor Cinderella, she endured their abuse day after day until, one day, she was visited by her fairy godmother who transformed her into a dazzling bachelorette who was sure to steal the eyes of the prince.

To make a long story short, Cinderella wore glass slippers to the prince's ball, one of which she lost while evading the prince—she had to hurry up and make it home before the fairy godmother's spell lifted and her beautiful gown transformed back into rags. Of course, the prince tracked her down using the glass slipper she lost; he then asked her for her hand in marriage, and the two of them rode off into the sunset where they lived happily ever after.

The end.

Well, that may have been the end of that story, but that's not how marriage works. In fact, if I were to pick up the story of Cinderella after her wedding to the prince and look at their marriage several years later, I guarantee you it wouldn't be a fairytale. It might go a little something like this: Cinderella and her husband, Prince Charming, began arguing more and more over little things. Having a hard time seeing eye-to-eye, the two of them had to see a marriage counselor to teach them better conflict/resolution skills. Cinderella complained during a session about her husband's busy schedule—the fact that he hardly spends time with her. The kids are driving the maids crazy. Her husband's morning breath can be unbearable at times. Her mother-in-law still treats her cold. She even overheard her mother-in-law telling her husband, "You could have done a lot better than that—a peasant girl. You can take a girl out of the fields, but you can't take the fields out of a girl. I wish you would have found a real Queen." That's only the beginning. The prince still has a kingdom to run, enemies to look out for, and a thousand-and-two little things to handle daily.

The honeymoon is over. Now the work has begun.

When we talk about marriage, might I remind you that it's work. Hard work. Just the willingness to forgive, to step outside of your own little world and venture into another's, the daily compromises one must make and constant attention to habits that irritate one's partner is a ton of work. And then add the kids. Busy schedules. Cooking. Cleaning. Stress from the job that you can't help but take home with you only to be met by a partner who's an already stressed out him or herself. The dog keeps pooping and peeing on the floor. Oh, God! Our daughter's recital is tonight?! I nearly forgot! Our son's game is this Saturday, but I have to rush and get him to practice and then rush back in time enough to finish dinner. Oh, God, I forgot the butter and cheese at the grocery store. This sounds like the life of a mother and wife. And you'd better not talk about a wife and mother who still has to hold down a job while dealing with the stress of navigating her own life while keeping an entire household in check.

No wonder so many married women will do anything and everything in their power to carve out a little me-time. That's why spas exist. That's why God created beaches and girls' trips.

The work of marriage can be overwhelming; it can crush you if you aren't ready for it. In the early stages of dating, you and your beau are getting to know one another, and you're busy enjoying the blissful feeling that falling-in-love brings; however, as scientists put it, after about two years or so, your brain returns to normal and you come down off of your chemical high, and then you start to notice things about the man you married that you couldn't see, or did see but chose to ignore, before. You notice his flaws, his shortcomings, the fact that he is not always the perfect gentleman, the fact that he's long ago stopped opening your car door for you and showering you with gifts. You notice that he doesn't cope too well with stress. He has a lot of baggage he brought with him into the relationship: ex-wife drama, baby-momma drama, debt, credit issues, trauma, ineffective conflict/resolution skills, and more. You notice that you also have much to work on. Both of you are flawed and have much to work on in your individual lives. That's work. This is where most newly—and even seasoned—married couples fail, and why they end up in the divorce court. They weren't ready for the work that marriage brings. No one ever told them what to expect. Well, I want to change that and tell you what to expect.

Expect changes. People change over time, and I'm not just talking about physically. He may have washboard abs today, but give it a few years. Like I mentioned earlier, you can't get caught up into the physical. Yes, looks are important, but they change. At some point in your relationship, there must develop a deeper bond that far transcends the physical in order for you and your spouse to remain together.

Expect a partner who's different from you. No, they're not going to like the same stuff you do. Your man may not like the same movies and shows you do, care much about lipstick and makeup, care about the things you and your girlfriends care about. He might like to play Call of Duty on the Playstation more than he enjoys cuddling on the couch and engaging in a hearty conversation. But you don't want him interfering with you when you're shopping for shoes and accessories in the mall either. You're supposed to be different—think differently, do things differently, and like different things. So don't act shocked that your partner is not you, and don't try to make them be like you. Let them be themselves, and you be yourself.

Also expect to be married to a person who has a ton of flaws...and some hidden issues too. They were a whole individual before they met you, which means they encountered other people and experienced traumatic situations before you even came on the scene. You might end up with a man whose heart has been abused, ripped out of his chest and stepped on by an ex-girlfriend or ex-wife, and now he has trust and commitment issues. That means you might have to give it a little time for him to let his guards down. Even worse, you might end up in a relationship with a narcissist. He may mistreat you and then blame you for the mistreatment as if he bears no responsibility for his actions. He may gaslight you until you think you're the crazy one. At that point, you'd better have a strong—and I mean STRONG—prayer life. In either case, just know that the person you're marrying is coming to the table with past pains and problems that have nothing to do with you, but can easily be triggered by your actions. Rather than run, you have to be willing to walk with that person through the valley of pain, and usher them by the hand into the arena of internal healing. That takes skill. That requires being able to overlook a lot of offence, forgive, study your partner, and discover the best way to handle them.

Lastly, expect the unexpected. What if your partner gets sick? Are you prepared to be a caretaker? Are you ready to change adult diapers? Are you ready to clean up behind a man who's lost the ability to do for himself?

Have you ever thought about those marriage vows: "For better or worse. In sickness and in health. For richer or poorer." If your man loses that good-paying job, will he lose you, too? Will you continue to be there for him, encouraging him, building him up, even showing him the utmost respect like the Bible instructs wives to do to their husbands?

Marriage is work, and it takes a special grace from God to succeed at it. But just know that all things are possible with God, and remember: "we can do all things through Him who strengthens us" (Philippians 4:13). When God brings two people together, He does so so that they might complete each other in certain ways. They will bring out the best in us and help us to accomplish the will of God for our lives.

Marriage is a beautiful thing, but it's work. Are you ready to work?

PRAYER

Heavenly Father, I thank you for the awesome plan you have for me, and I know that as a part of that plan you want to bless me with a wonderful prayer partner. Father, today I adjust my expectations so that they line up with your will and with reality. I thank you today for giving me an understanding that marriage isn't about having someone to serve me; it's about me learning to serve another. Give me a servant's heart. Teach me how to put the needs of another before my own. Teach me how to fight in the spirit over the husband you are giving me, how to pray over him and intercede for his breakthrough. Teach me how to be sensitive to his wants and needs and bring out the gift and purpose you've placed inside of him. Thank you for preparing me today to be the Queen my future King needs—the support system that he needs, the encourager he needs, the prayer partner he needs, the lover he needs, the helper he needs, and more. I pray this in Jesus name, amen.

DAY 13: AM I MENTALLY PREPARED FOR MARRIAGE?

Day 14

Kids, Blended Families, and Ex's

Okay, let's get real. Real real! Some blessings don't always come the way you like. They might come in packages you don't expect and with some extra stuff you aren't looking for. That's the case here. You found the man of your dreams. He's handsome, charming, has a good job, and he loves his momma. He fulfills all of your desires in a mate. And then, you discover that he has kids. And I'm not talking about babies either. I'm talking about teenagers, young adults. You go over to his house one day to meet them and they're all standing there with their arms folded, staring at you like you work for the IRS. The teenage daughter just rolled her eyes at you—you wish you could snatch them out of her head and shove them into her smart aleck mouth. His son looks at you like you're a disease and wonders why you're standing in their house—after all, it should be his biological mother standing there, not you. That's what he's thinking and feeling. Even the dog looks disturbed that you're there.

Trust me, this is a nightmare scenario for most single women. And let me add a little more on for you. Your dream guy's ex-wife is still in the picture. She's somewhere, lurking not far away, probably watching you through a pair of binoculars. Well, maybe she's not crazy, or at least that crazy, but she's still a mother bear who's highly protective of her cubs. And you're around her cubs. That's just more drama to deal with.

As a pastor, I've counseled couples living with blended families, and this is the type of scenario I've run across so many times. The husband or wife entering into the lives of their partner's children is treated like an outsider, and they feel it strongly. They have to experience the cold winds of rejection from their spouse's children who don't want them in their lives. In these situations, the incoming partner has two options: either work to form a bond with their spouse's children, or start World War 3 with their spouse's kids, which would be a bad idea. Or there's a third option: walk away from the relationship altogether. Should they choose to stay, they have to face the reality that they may be the object of contempt for a while. Despite their best efforts to bond with their spouse's kids, they may still face rejection. It doesn't matter how many gifts they buy the kids or how much money they give them, they still get treated coldly.

Should you ever end up in this situation, it's important to remember that you're not her problem. Don't take it personally. Don't feel any way responsible for your partner's kids' feelings towards you. They may feel contemptuous towards you only because of their anger over their parents' split; you just happen to get caught in the crossfires.

Children eventually grow up. They eventually leave the nest—well, most of them do. Once gone, they move on with their lives. They marry, have kids, start careers, and then stop by only on special holidays to see you and to eat up all of your food. Therefore, don't allow your kids to rob you of your personal happiness if you're with a man who loves and respects you and your children, one who was sent into your life by God to be a blessing to you. Teach your children to respect your man. That's your responsibility. You train them to respect their teachers and other authority figures, the same should apply in the home. It's about discipline, and the responsibility to discipline children falls on the parent.

Now you can't force your children to like or love someone, and neither should you try to make them accept someone new in your life. Your kids are entitled to their feelings. It may take them a while to warm up to the idea that there's a new man in their lives. Just give them time. They have to be willing to trust this new individual for themselves before they embrace him. Your new man has to be willing to build a relationship with your kids, which takes time to do. He must be patient, understanding, gentle, and humble. He cannot walk through the door demanding that your kids call him dad. That's an indicative of a controlling individual, the type of man you don't want in your life. But if he's the right type of man, the type of man that God has for you, he'll operate in the Fruit of the Spirit (Galatians 5:22-23), which is the character of God. With godly character, he'll enhance your life and respect your children, and add value to the entire household rather than cause division and chaos. And the same applies to you if you're the woman entering into the life of a man who already has kids—you'll be a blessing in that household rather than a source of destruction.

If you're in a blended family, it's your partner's responsibility to train their children to respect you. You shouldn't have to feel as if you're all alone, being left to defend yourself. That isn't your job. Your partner still has to be a parent. They wouldn't let their kids disrespect the teachers at their schools, and neither should they allow their kids to disrespect their new beau at home. The kids don't have to like you, but they do have to respect their parent's decision. Respect and manners are a part of what we call home-training. Parents who fail to teach their children home-training set their children up for failure in life; they let their kids run over them and enable destructive behaviors. That reveals a lot about your partner: they might not share the same belief system you have. For example, the Bible says, "Spare the rod, spoil the child" (Proverbs 13:24). That same verse tells us the parent that refuses to chastise their child hates their child. These child-rearing principles are biblically-based; however, if you are in a relationship with someone who doesn't share your principles and value system, that's an even bigger problem. For the Bible declares, "Can two people walk together without agreeing on the direction?" (Amos 3:3, NLT). It's important that before you get married, you find out if you and your partner are going in the same direction and share the same morals and values.

In a marriage, it's important that you and your spouse present a unified front before the kids. When they see the two of you on one accord, they will be less inclined to disrespect your partner. On the other hand, if they sense that you don't respect your partner's authority in the relationship, they'll feel emboldened and empowered to disrespect your partner. When this begins to happen, the relationship is headed for disaster.

I can't stress this enough! Have the conversation with your partner about children and child-rearing before you get married; actually, do this before you bring your new man home to meet the kids. Don't bring home someone that isn't prepared to deal with your kids. If you bring a man into your kids' lives who isn't ready for children, he will most likely try to drive a wedge between you and your kids, and if that relationship doesn't work out, you will be faced with repairing the broken relationship with, and regain the trust of, your own children. Don't be so quick to take a man home until you discover what type of man he is. You want to know whether or not he's a good fit for you and your children.

Lastly, I can't let you go without addressing the elephant in most rooms: the ex. If you are in a relationship with a man who has an ex that's still around, you have to be prepared to deal with the reality that his children will most likely never choose you over their biological mother and their mom will probably view you as competition in the lives of her children. It's important that you reassure your man's kids that you're not trying to replace their mom, and that you honor their mom regardless of how rude she may be. Don't try to insert yourself in the middle of their business. Don't try to insert yourself in the middle of your partner and his ex's business either. Be there for your man and realize that this is a situation that existed long before you came around. Trust your partner to do the right thing. And if he can't seem to let his ex go, then it may be time for you to leave. He must be sure of what he wants—and if it's not you, then you don't need to hang around.

PRAYER

Heavenly Father, I thank you today for the wisdom and the patience to deal with a blended family. Jesus, you were patient with me. You put up with me and allowed me to make mistakes without discarding me. I thank you for giving me the patience to deal with stepsons and step-daughters, in-laws and ex-spouses. I thank you for giving me the right words to say to them, the right approach to take with them, and the wisdom to deal with every situation that arises. I pray for my partner or future partner and their offspring, and I declare, Holy Spirit, they are yours. Move in their lives like never before and have your way. I come against every spirit that brings division, contention, and strife, and declare today that the divine order of God rest, rule, and reign in our blended household, in Jesus name, amen.

DAY 15

MONEY & DEBT

O KAY, I KNOW THIS ISN'T THE MOST POPULAR conversation, but it's important. Again, as I stated in an earlier section, the honeymoon phase will eventually end and life will kick in. That's when the arguments usually come, the fights emerge, the problems surface. That's when you realize what you stepped into. That's when you discover the amount of debt your partner has or how bad their credit score is. That's when you notice they don't like to pay bills or they have habits that drain the family finances. When your stomach is growling because there's no food in the refrigerator and there's no money to buy food because your partner spent all of the money on addictions or useless things, I guarantee you that sex is the last thing on your mind. The only thing you'll want to do is wring your partner's neck.

As I stated in an earlier section, it is not God's will for us to remain in debt. Debt is a form of slavery. Whether you're indebted to the bank, the government, a lending institution, or family and friends, God wants you to get out of debt because it will prevent you from walking in the freedom and boldness of the Lord like you're supposed to. God doesn't want you to max out your credit cards and spending impulsively as if the world is about to come to an end if you don't buy that dress. He gave you the gift of self-control. He doesn't want you making an idol out of money either, hoarding it and holding on to it for dear life. He wants you to obey His instructions regarding money and honor Him with your finances.

It's critical that you study your partner's spending habits and get to know their beliefs about money before jumping into a marriage with them. The Bible talks a lot about money, in particular, stewardship. Oftentimes, people will pray to God for more money while mishandling the finances He's already given to them; this is a sign of bad stewardship. Proper stewardship begins with a fundamental belief, one that must be the foundation for your marriage: God is our source. You and your partner need to see God as the source of your finances, and all other blessings you enjoy. With that being on the forefronts of your minds, you will have a sense of accountability towards God in all that you do, especially when it comes to your handling of money. You'd ask yourself, Would God want me to pay these bills and settle my debts? Would God want me to be fair and honest with my money by paying people back that I owe? Would God want me to spend my money on personal wants while neglecting household needs? Would God want me to waste money? Would God want me to make bad financial investments or invest financially into immoral things? Does God want me to honor Him with my tithes and sow into the things of His Kingdom?

When we walk in the fear of the Lord and reverence

Him as the source of our finances and blessings, we'll strive to honor Him and do that which is right in His eyes. That's why the Bible has over two-thousands verses on money—it's revealing to us that a person's nature and character is displayed in their handling of money. Or said another way, Jesus put it this way: "For where your treasure is, there your heart will be also" (Matthew 6:21, NIV). You can tell where a man's heart is by where he invests his money, time, and energy. It's easy to say you love God and your family, but talk is cheap. The Apostle Paul, when challenging the Christians in Corinth, explained to them that their financial support of the church allows them to "prove the sincerity of your love" (2 Corinthians 8:8). Nothing proves your love more than the selfless act of giving that which is most valuable, needed, and important in your life: your money. That's why God tests us with money.

Again, money is important in marriage. Should you marry someone who doesn't have godly principles and values, they'll more than likely misuse money. Some may use money as a tool to dominate and control you while others may use money as a tool to manipulate others. Some may misuse money and drive up debt because they're impatient, inconsiderate, selfish, and desperate to get rich quick. Some may lose money because they're arrogant, headstrong, and addicted to substances and pleasure. Knowing your partner's spending habits reveals to you where their heart is and what their principles and values are; it reveals to you their level of integrity and honesty, all of which you'll want to know before you tie the knot with them.

I can't overstate the importance of becoming financially responsible and choosing a partner who's financially responsible. After the wedding, that's when the marriage begins, and it's during this phase that couples are faced with certain realities. For example, one partner is faced with their partner's debt. Couples find themselves in a bind because they didn't think about things such as life insurance. I know, no one wants to think about tragedy and loss. No one wants to imagine the possibility that they might lose their partner to an untimely death. We all like to think that we'll grow old with our chosen partners and pass away quietly in the night together like that couple from the movie The Notebook—sleeping side by side, holding one another while drifting peacefully into eternity. However, as I experienced, loss can come at unexpected times and snatch your partner away. After the untimely death of my late husband, I had to think about things I didn't want to consider when I first got married. Discuss early on in your relationship things such as a will, estate planning and life insurance.

PRAYER

Heavenly Father, thank you for every good and perfect gift you've provided me. I thank you for your financial blessings over my life. Father, teach me how to honor you with my finances and make money my servant rather than my master. You said in your Word that man cannot serve two masters; therefore, I denounce the god of money (Mammon) and receive your rule and lordship over my financial life. I will honor you with my tithes and sow seed into your Kingdom. I will be a financial blessing to your house and give you the glory for every financial blessing and breakthrough I receive in my life. Help me to walk in your character so that I may do right by others regarding finances. Father, I thank you again that I am not called to a life of lack, debt, and slavery; therefore, give me wisdom and understanding so that I can eliminate all debts owed and walk in the financial prosperity you've predestined for my life. I pray this in Jesus name, amen.

DAY 16

WHAT'S MY TYPE?

BEFORE YOU GET EXCITED OVER THE IDEA OF finding your King and getting married, I'd strongly advise you to take some time to find out what you want in a partner. You need to find out what's your type. What type of man are you looking for—and make no mistake about it, all men are not the same. You need to know what your wants, desires, preferences, and deal-breakers are. What are you willing and unwilling to live with? What is pleasing and attractive to you?

World-renown psychologist and author, Dr. Gary Chapman, in his bestselling book The 5 Love Languages, takes readers on a journey within themselves, helping them to discover things about themselves they might have overlooked. He helps readers to discover their own preferences when it comes to the way they want to be loved. What does love look like and feel like to you? What makes you feel loved? What makes you feel valued? Do you like to be touched (hugging, caressing, cuddling)? Do you love to hear people affirm you with uplifting and encouraging words? Do you like to be praised? Do you prefer to have a man who brings home gifts frequently as an expression of his love? What's your preference? Do you feel loved when someone spends money on you and takes you out on nice dates? Or would you prefer to have a partner who shares in the housework, helping you to cook and clean? What turns you on the most? You need to know what you like so you won't settle for someone that won't love you the way you want to be loved. This is important because, as time progresses, your unmet needs and desires will become an issue in your marriage; they will become a source of contention and even resentment if continually overlooked and unmet.

Have you considered or even discovered the things that make you happy and turn you on? Often times, we focus only on the outer appearance of a mate, but we don't think about the things that create a strong sense of chemistry: things such as shared interests, similar goals in life, and shared experiences and beliefs. You need to think about every aspect of a mate—how you want them to serve you. That's what a relationship is: two people serving each other. If you don't know how you want to be served, this will discourage and frustrate your partner, causing them to believe you are not happy with them. We do things for those we love, not so that they can repay us, but because we gain pleasure from making them happy. We are eager to serve and please those we love. The best way to make your partner feel special is to allow them to serve you, and to tell them they are doing a good job at it. Remember, a man simply wants to feel appreciated. He works from sun up to sundown so that he can see his family happy; he just wants to be shown appreciation so that he can know he's doing a good job. Let your partner know what your preferences are concerning how you want to be served.

I'm not encouraging you to be selfish, but I'm not suggesting that you put your wants and needs on the back-burner either. You have the right to be picky, to be choosy as long as you don't become irrational and hold unreasonable expectations. No one is perfect. You are not going to find a perfect guy. You may find a man who is good in one area but not as good in another area. For example, you may find a man who is a good provider, but needs help in the romance department. Or he may be good in the romance department, but he doesn't like to help out around the house. Or he may treat you like a Queen and work hard and even help out around the house, but he might not make a lot of money. There isn't a perfect man. And you are not perfect either. You might not have everything the man of your dreams is looking for in a partner either. He might want a woman with a perfect body; a woman who will cook breakfast, lunch, and dinner daily; a woman who will never tell him "no" in the bedroom, who never complains, who is 100% obedient, and who wakes up every morning looking like an airbrushed model out of a Victoria's Secret catalogue and waits on him hand-and-foot throughout the day. Oh, and she has perfect credit, doesn't want to spend any money, loves football, and doesn't have any past baggage. Of course, if a man is searching for that kind of woman, good luck finding her because...she doesn't exist.

Make sure your expectations are reasonable. And don't just expect the good either. Anticipate the bad, too. Know that the man God has for you will come with flaws and have areas in his life where improvements are needed. He will come with baggage, but that is what will strengthen the relationship: when you and your partner become totally transparent with one another and help each other heal from past wounds.

You might just have a diamond in the rough on your hands. Don't throw that jewel of a man away because he has dirt on him and doesn't appear to be much right now. If you stick with him and handle him properly, becoming an instrument of healing in his life rather than being an instrument of destruction, he might just turn into the man of your dreams. He may look like a frog today, but a kiss from the right woman will transform him into the royalty he was predestined by God to be.

So, yes, be picky and choosy, but most of all, be Spirit-led.

PRAYER

Heavenly Father, thank you for your presence in my life. I thank you for creating me in your image and likeness, and for also making me unique. You have endowed me with gifts, talents, and abilities. You have also birthed within me desires and preferences regarding relationships. Today, I surrender my heart, mind, body and soul to you. Let my desires align with your will for my life. Give me a clean heart and the right spirit. Take out of me any desire that is out of alignment with your will for me.

Father, guide my expectations concerning relationships. Give me the wisdom to hold the right expectations of others, especially the partner you have chosen for me, and help me to walk in compassion and prudence. I thank you for what you are doing inside of me and are getting ready to do in my life. It's in Jesus name I pray, amen.

____

____

____

____

____

____

____

____

____

____

____

____

Healing From The Loss Of A Loved-One

"Mrs. Thomas, before you go into the room, we want you to know we have our best medical team working on your husband." That's what I remember hearing as I frantically ran into the hospital shortly after the EMT took him there. As I entered behind the door, there were so many people working on my husband. Someone guided me to his side to hold his hand and pulled up a chair. I felt it on the back of my leg but I was in so much shock I couldn't sit down. Then I heard a long beep come from the medical equipment they attached to my husband. I would eventually discover it's what they call a "flat line," which means the patients heart has stopped. Then I heard the Doctor utter the time, which I realized shortly afterwards was the time of my husband's death. How did all of this happen to a healthy, vibrant man who had no history of medical challenges? I was searching for answers all while grieving the one I lost and loved so dearly.

Some people have experienced the death of a spouse or the breakup of a relationship they have invested their time, resources, and hearts in. Healing from these types of losses take time. The entanglement that occurred in that relationship took place over a long period of time, therefore, it will take time for you to heal and even adjust to life without that person. However, time does heal all wounds, especially emotional wounds. But this is only if you are intentional about getting healed. I knew I had to seek emotional healing from the death of my late husband if I was to ever re-marry. I knew I couldn't expect my future King to carry the burden of grief from my past relationship. That would be unfair of me to place such a burden on his shoulders.

I began working on my healing process; this meant I had to get grief counseling so that I could understand what I was experiencing emotionally. I needed to process the loss and the feelings I was experiencing. Again, whether it's a sudden loss, a breakup, or a divorce, don't try to heal yourself. Don't sit around and think that the pain will just go away eventually and then you'll feel better. Find a therapist or support group that can help you walk through the healing process.

Today's prayer will focus on healing from a loss or a breakup. Your future King deserves the best version of you. So while you are waiting for him, you are being healed in those deep places of your heart.

PRAYER

Dear Heavenly Father, I thank you that you see everything. You see the pain in my heart and see every tear that falls from my eyes. You said you are close to the broken-hearted. Father, I know that all things work together for the good of them who love you and are called according to your purpose. Even my pain is working together for my good. Even the tragedy I experienced is working together for my good. I may not understand everything, but as your Word declares in Proverbs 3:5-6, "Trust in the LORD with all your heart; do not depend on your own understanding. Seek his will in all you do, and he will show you which path to take" (NLT). I surrender my heart and mind to you and abandon my understanding. I trust your will and judgment, knowing that you are working behind the scenes to do something incredible in my life. You give me beauty for ashes. You have placed on me the garment of praise in place of the garment of heaviness and depression. I declare and decree that my tomorrow is brighter than ever because I trust in you and I have placed my life in your hands. Today, I bind the spirit of grief and acknowledge the Holy Spirit as my source and my strength. Today, I cast down every lie of the enemy that tells me I am alone, and that I will never experience love and happiness in a loving and fulfilling relationship. Father, you know what I need, and you have already made arrangements for my future mate. I thank you for healing my heart this day, in Jesus name, amen.

____

____

____

____

____

____

____

DAY 18

DO NOT SETTLE

NOT EVERYONE MARRIES FOR THE SAME reason. It is assumed that everyone marries out of love; we marry our soulmates so that we can settle down and feel fulfilled; however, that's not actually the case. Some people marry for financial reasons, and some marry out of the pressure placed on them by their family, friends, and community. Of course, these are the wrong reasons to get married, but they are common reasons.

Growing up, I've seen plenty of guys and girls get married due to outside pressure. It's not that the parties involved in the marriage held a deep, genuine love for one another; in some cases, they barely liked each other; however, they tied the knot anyway. Why? Because their family members, friends, church members, and loved-ones pressured them to. And sadly, many couples remained married only because of external factors: they built a business together, served in leadership together, built a reputation around their marriage, felt the need to appear happy to save their ministry, and more. These people remained in loveless, sexless, passionless, unhappy and unfulfilling marriages out of fear. They suffered in silence behind closed doors. Many of them suffering physical abuse. They used as their mantra to keep their misery hidden: "What goes on in this house stays in this house."

As a child, I remember my mother had a friend that was in an abusive marriage. Her husband verbally and physically abused her, and most times, he did it in front of their son who was the same age as me. She was a very pretty woman, but the words he spoke over her made her feel less than her worth. In front of family and friends he seemed to be the life of the party: very outgoing, outspoken and friendly. But behind closed doors he was a monster.

I once overheard her telling my mother how he treated her and physically assaulted her. Though I was just a child, it enraged me, and I spoke up and told her that wasn't right. My mom immediately reminded me that I was a child and to get out of grown folks' conversations. Well, I didn't say anything else, but I never saw him the same way again. Whenever they would come around I would see through him; I would see through his fake smile and demeanor. I could see she was always on eggshells, jumping and flinching every time he touched her. Their son was starting to take on his father's personality towards her, disrespectfully speaking to her, his mother.

One day she reached a breaking point and couldn't take his abuse any longer. She fled to my house to seek safety with my mom. I remember her being so afraid that her husband would find out where she was and try to hurt her. Everyone knew to tell him she wasn't at our house if he called. Then some time had passed, and like children who can be forgetful, I forgot she wasn't supposed to be at our house when he called. One day, he caught me off guard and called asking for her. I said, "Hold on, here she is." It was at that moment I remembered I wasn't supposed to say that. She immediately packed up and left our house before her husband could come by to find her.

What happened to my mother's dear, sweet friend? She settled for a man who could never genuinely love her like she desired and deserved, and she ended up living on the run like a fugitive. She couldn't be stable on a job because he was stalking her. She couldn't be in a stable living arrangements because he would find her. Their son lacked stability in his childhood—being uprooted from one school after another, constantly moving so his father wouldn't find them.

This might be hard to imagine, but people live like that every day, which is unfortunate.

Look, if you're unhappy in your relationship while dating, you'll be unhappy in it after getting married. If you're experiencing abuse now while dating, you'll experience more abuse after getting married. Don't settle! Don't assume that what you have is the best you can do and choose to just live with it. You deserve the best. You deserve better.

Look at your current dating situation and ask yourself if you are happy. If not, then it is time to move on. Don't settle and tie yourself down with someone you already have doubts about. Don't marry someone out of pity—you feel sorry for them and fear that they will hurt themselves and/or others if you leave them. If you marry for that reason, you will remain in bondage for the rest of your life, being blackmailed into submission by a person's constant threat of self-harm. You will be miserable. That's not God's will.

He wants you to be happy, to be in a loving and fulfilling relationship. He never advocates getting into and remaining in a relationship out of fear, pity, desperation, anger, remorse, and due to outside pressure. That is bondage, and God is not one to entangle us in slavery.

Don't settle. Let God bless you with his best. Expect the best. You deserve it.

PRAYER

Dear Heavenly Father, I thank you for being a good father, one who only desires the best for his children. I'm your child, therefore, I know that you have my interests at heart and desire the best for me. You never do anything halfway. You always strive in the attitude of excellence and perfection. You have the perfect mate for me. You have the best in mind for me. Why? It is because I'm your child. It is your good pleasure to bless me with my heart's desires. As your Word declares, when I delight myself in you, you will give me my heart's desires (Psalm 34). Father, I thank you that you are sending me a King that will honor and respect me, treat me like a Queen, meet my physical, emotional, and psychological needs, stand with me in prayer, and fulfill me in every way. You desire that I be happy. Give me wisdom. Speak to my heart. I surrender to your will, your guidance and leadership. I lean not to my own understanding, but ask that you speak to me today concerning your will. Guide my steps so that I don't settle with anyone and anything that is outside of your will for my life. I thank you for the gifts of wisdom and discernment today, in Jesus' name, amen.

DAY 19

LONELY VERSES BEING ALONE

THERE IS A DIFFERENCE BETWEEN BEING lonely and being alone. The difference is simple: being lonely is a state of mind; being alone is a physical state. There are plenty of people who are not alone, but they feel lonely. They are surrounded by family and friends but still feel lonely. They can sit in a crowded room at a party surrounded by a sea of people and still feel lonely. Why? It's because loneliness is a state of mind. They don't know how to connect with people. They are afraid to open their mouths and speak to others. They fear rejection, and hence, avoid interactions with others at all cost. They bottle up thoughts and feelings within and sit in silence, suffering in their minds rather than connecting with others.

It's possible to be locked up in a mental prison where you fear being around people, where you fear opening up to people and building close relationships with them. Usually, loneliness is associated with anxiety and depression. Lonely people tend to shy away from relationships and retreat into isolation, but isolation only serves the purpose of reinforc-ing the idea in their minds that nobody wants to be around them. That's not true, but that's what they tell themselves.

The Bible says, "A man who has friends must him-self be friendly..." (Proverbs 18:24, NKJV). Oftentimes, lonely people refuse to reach out to others to form connec-tions, which makes others think they prefer to be left alone. They may secretly long to connect with others, but their actions give off the wrong signal.

Truth be told, many of us want a King to come and find us, to make the first move and chase us down; howev-er, in reality, we have to be willing to invite men to the table. We have to demonstrate an interest in getting involved in a relationship. If a man approaches you and you lift your nose up at him and act like you're not interested, he's going to assume you're not interested and move on. A man won't chase after a woman who puts out the signal that she's not interested. Smile. Be friendly. You might even have to make the first move: say something to him first, approach him and strike up a conversation, let him know that you're interested in him. No, that's not the same as chasing him down; that's simply showing an interest and then letting him decide whether or not he wants to pursue that avenue with you. You can't sit around with a "Do Not Disturb" sign on your face and expect to land a partner. It doesn't work that way. Show yourself friendly first. Step outside of your comfort-zone and seek after a connection.

Regarding being alone, that's not a bad thing if you look at it correctly. Being alone just means you have more time to devote to God and the development of self. It means you have fewer distractions and obligations pulling you away from that which is most important in life. It's possible to be alone and not feel lonely. You can actually enjoy being alone: enjoy finding yourself, enjoy developing yourself in the areas you need building, enjoy learning new skills and new things about yourself and the world, enjoy treating yourself without the hassle of having to accommodate someone else in the process. How great is that? To be able to do what you want to do without waiting on someone else. To be able to go where you want to go without needing someone else's permission. The freedom to build or rebuild your own world from the ground up. Being alone is an advantage that allows us to put things in proper perspective and make the changes we need to make in our lives in order to position ourselves for bigger, better, and greater.

Being alone is right where you need to be to prepare yourself for your future King. While alone, this is the opportunity to work on yourself...and even deal with the internal issues that breed the feeling of loneliness. Embrace this time. Spend this time drawing closer to God so that He can heal you from the emotional, psychological, and spiritual wounds that have impacted your life for years.

PRAYER

Dear Heavenly Father, I thank you that you are an ever-present help in the time of need. You said you will never leave nor forsake me. You are always present with me. Your angels stand guard around me daily. I am never alone. Never! Today, pour out your presence and love all over me and shower me with your favor. I open myself to you today. Father, I acknowledge that any and all feelings of loneliness and depression are from Satan, not you. The thief sent them my way. He lied to me and told me that I am unlovable, that nobody wants to be close to me, that I will mess up every good thing that comes my way. These are all lies. You did not give me a spirit of fear, but of love, power, and a sound mind. Today, I cast down the fear of rejection. I cast down ever lie told to me by the spirit of fear. I am not less than or unworthy. I am worthy, likable, lovable, smart, fun to be around, uplifting and encouraging, attractive, and valuable. I love who you made me and value myself—you didn't make a mistake when you made me. During my times of aloneness, I will draw even closer to you. I thank you for those times in my life. I will not only value and appreciate them, but take advantage of them for my benefit. I will use them to spend more time with you, to allow you to examine me and deal with the issues of my heart. I will take those times and use them to grow spiritually and develop personally. I thank you for this, in Jesus' name I pray, amen.

Day 20

Being Unequally Yoked

In 2 Corinthians 6:14, we find these words: "Be ye not unequally yoked together with unbelievers: for what fellowship hath righteousness with unrighteousness? and what communion hath light with darkness? And what concord hath Christ with Belial? or what part hath he that believeth with an infidel? And what agreement hath the temple of God with idols? for ye are the temple of the living God; as God hath said, I will dwell in them, and walk in them; and I will be their God, and they shall be my people." In this passage of Scripture, the Apostle Paul urges us as Believers to avoid entering into partnerships with people whose hearts and minds are pointed in the opposite direction from ours. Ignoring this warning only leads to heartache and disappointment.

A yoke was a device used by farmers. They would place this wooden device around the necks of oxen to bind them together as depicted in the photograph below:

This wooden device bound the animals together, preventing them from going their separate ways. When yoked with someone, that means you have entered into an agreement with them that forces you to be with them. You have obligated yourself to that person or their cause and are stuck. That's why the Bible tells us to be careful with our words—to avoid making vows and commitments without praying and being Spirit-led first. Don't obligate yourself to anyone and anything without first getting the green light from the Holy Spirit. If it doesn't sit well with your soul and you don't feel good about someone or something, don't enter into a commitment with that person or thing. Opening your mouth and speaking too soon will cause you to be "trapped by what you said, ensnared by the words of your mouth" (Proverbs 6:2, NIV).

It's okay to give yourself time to think about things before deciding to commit or not commit. Don't let anyone pressure you into a commitment. And you don't have to provide an answer a that very moment. Make people respect you by realizing they can't pressure you into anything, especially something you don't feel comfortable about or don't want to do. And if they're trying to pressure you, realize they have ulterior motives.

Before committing yourself to someone, find out where their head and heart is. Find out if they have a genuine relationship with God. Find out if they share your same principles and values. Find out if they want the same things you want in life. This is critically important because once you say "I do" you have just yoked yourself with that person. And if they are going in one direction and you are going in another direction, that yoke will serve as a bondage tying you to something that's a hindrance in your life. You will exert unnecessary energy and find yourself embroiled in constant struggles throughout your relationship.

Now, I do realize that some people, when they first get married, they are in the same place mentally, emotionally, and spiritually; however, as time progresses, one person may start to grow and mature mentally, emotionally, and spiritually while the other person may not. I see and hear this a lot from couples: The wife is upset because she wants to change and draw closer to God, so she's attending church more, praying, and reading her Bible; her husband, on the other hand, still wants to party, drink, smoke, hang out in the clubs and at bars, and do the same things they did earlier in their relationship. Now the wife is frustrated with her husband and wants to leave him, and she'll even quote 2 Corinthians 6:14 as justification for her disrespect towards him and disengagement from their marriage. That is wrong. Just read 1 Corinthians 7:12-16, which tells us,

> "Now, I will speak to the rest of you, though I do not have a direct command from the Lord. If a Christian man has a wife who is not a believer and she is willing to continue living with him, he must not leave her. And if a Christian woman has a husband who is not a believer and he is willing to continue living with her, she must not leave him. For the Christian wife brings holiness to her marriage, and the Christian husband brings holiness to his marriage. Otherwise, your children would not be holy, but now they are holy. (But if the husband or wife who isn't a believer insists on leaving, let them go. In such cases the Christian husband or wife is no longer bound to the other, for God has called you to live in peace.) Don't you wives realize that your husbands might be saved because of you? And don't you husbands realize that your wives might be saved because of you?" (NLT)

No, God doesn't want you to up and leave cold turkey just because your spouse isn't growing fast enough in your eyes...or growing spiritually at all. You yoked yourself with him, so now you must labor in prayer and fasting and godly wisdom to help bring him into the light. And if he decides to leave because he doesn't like the change he sees in you, Paul said let him leave and then move on with your life. But your job is to evangelize your spouse using the love and wisdom of God.

Peter talked about wives who have unbelieving husbands in 1 Peter 3:1-6. He wrote,

"In the same way, you wives must accept the authority of your husbands. Then, even if some refuse to obey the Good News, your godly lives will speak to them without any words. They will be won over by observing your pure and reverent lives. Don't be concerned about the outward beauty of fancy hairstyles, expensive jewelry, or beautiful clothes. You should clothe yourselves instead with the beauty that comes from within, the unfading beauty of a gentle and quiet spirit, which is so precious to God. This is how the holy women of old made themselves beautiful. They trusted God and accepted the authority of their husbands. For instance, Sarah obeyed her husband, Abraham, and called him her master. You are her daughters when you do what is right without fear of what your husbands might do."

Notice that your respect towards that man, your honoring him, your "gentle and quite spirit" and willingness to treat him like a King even when he's acting like a kid, is how the Bible says you are supposed to evangelize your husband "without [saying] any words". Being a witness to your husband doesn't entail beating him upside the head with the Bible and shaming him to death; it entails showing him honor and respect and loving him with the love of

God even though he doesn't deserve it. Through this, you will melt the hardness around his heart. That is now your mission if you are already married. But if you are still single, you have the option of vetting more carefully your chosen mate to find out if they are someone you should "yoke" up with. You have the freedom to walk away from a potentially bad and disastrous situation.

Ask questions. Keep your eyes open. Examine your partner to see if their principles, morals and values align with yours—more importantly, if they align with God's. If they don't then that's not someone you should partner with.

PRAYER

Dear Heavenly Father, your Word instructs me not to enter into partnership with someone whose morals, principles, and values don't align with yours. You warned me not to be unequally yoked with someone who wants to follow after darkness while I'm following after the light. Father, give me the strength and the wisdom to walk away from any person or thing that is not right for me according to your will and plan for my life. Forgive me if I have spoken any words out of haste and made commitments to people and things I am not supposed to be a part of. Give me the wisdom to get out of these agreements. Open up a door for me to walk away. And guide my tongue through wisdom and prudence so that I don't speak before I think and before I consult you. And Father, give me the wisdom to deal with those you won't remove from my life. Help me to be a light unto them so that they will be influenced by your presence in my life. Help me to love them as you love me. I thank you for guiding my steps today and forevermore, in Jesus' name, amen.

FUTURE KING, I'M PRAYING FOR YOU

Dear Heavenly Father, I thank you for my future King. I thank you that you have already called him by name and set him aside for me. You are the one directing our steps, causing us to cross paths. I thank you for him, Father. I thank you that he is a man of strength, courage, a man who loves you and seeks to do your will. I thank you that my future King is a man of wisdom. He is diligent in that which you have called him to. He walks in his divine purpose. He turns to you for guidance. He is a man of God. I thank you Heavenly Father that my future King is on the way, and that through your discernment I will recognize him when he comes. I thank you that my future King and I will walk in agreement to fulfill your will for our lives. Today, I cast down every plan of the enemy to sabotage my relationship with my future King. I come against every hindering spirit on assignment to divert our paths from one another. I come against every attempt of the enemy to cause division in our union. I declare and decree today that there will be peace in our home, unity in our union, and that we will honor our covenant made before you. Heavenly Father, I thank you for my future King, and I thank you that you are preparing me to be his future Queen. Thank you for healing me from every open wound in my heart. I denounce every inner vow I have made out of frustration, anger, and confusion. I repent of them. I open my heart for you to fill it. I choose to walk in fear no longer. I choose to open my heart to love. I choose to walk in forgiveness rather than harboring anger and resentment in my heart towards my future King for mistakes he will make. And I thank you Father that he will walk in forgiveness towards me for the future mistakes I will make also. Father, I pray that you will place righteous voices around my future King and me. Let him be surrounded by wise counsel today. Let my ears only be attuned to those who are speaking your wisdom. I thank you, Father, for the future King who is entering my life. I thank you that we are custom-made for each other and that we will be a source of support and happiness in each other's lives. I thank you Father for what you are doing and are about to do in my life. I receive the King you have for me today, in Jesus' name, amen.

About The Author

Marlyn S. Thomas is the Senior Pastor and Founder at Life Line Family Worship Center in Fayetteville, GA. She holds an earned Doctorate Degree in Theology and two Honorary Doctorates. Pastoring for over 18 years, Bishop Thomas has seen the 'hand of God' rest mightily upon her ministry. She enjoys the ministry and continues to operate in the prophetic anointing.

Bishop Thomas is a Gospel recording artist, author, the host of *Motivation Moment With Marlyn Show*, philanthropist, and sought after speaker.

Widowed in her late 40's, she felt called by God to pin this book to help single women that desire to be married.

Bishop Thomas has one adult son, Kenny Gaines, and is a Spiritual Mother to many.

She is affectionately known as the 'Winning Bishop' because she's always motivating people to WIN!

Bishop Thomas' life mantra is, "Jesus lives in me, I can WIN with the hand I'm dealt!"

To contact the author, go to
www.MotivationWithDrMarlyn.com
win@motivationwithdrmarlyn.com
Facebook: Marlyn S Thomas
Instagram: @BishopMarlynThomas